THE BIG
DINOSAUR
BOOK

CHANCELLOR
PRESS

An Hachette UK Company
www.hachette.co.uk

Published in 2015 by Chancellor Press, an imprint
of Bounty Books,
a division of Octopus Publishing Group Ltd
Carmelite House
50 Victoria Embankment
London, EC4Y 0DZ
www.octopusbooks.co.uk

ISBN: 978-0-75373-005-8

A CIP catalogue record for this book is
available from the British Library

Printed and bound in China

10 9 8 7 6 5 4 3 2 1

Contents

Introduction

People have always been fascinated by dinosaurs! From the earliest discoveries of dinosaur bones in the mid-19th century, children and adults alike have wanted to read all about these giant creatures: where they lived, what they ate, what they looked like and how they were eventually wiped out. This book provides a comprehensive look at the world of the dinosaurs from both a historical and a scientific viewpoint. Not only does it investigate the lives of the major dinosaurs from the Triassic, Jurassic and Cretaceous periods, but also those of other ancient reptiles inhabiting the Earth at that time.

History of Palaeontology

For many hundreds of years, people were fascinated by the strange bones they found poking out from cliffs and beaches. But it was not until the 19th century that scientists began to try to work out what these fossils might actually mean. Today, palaeontologists know that they were the bones of dinosaurs and have pieced together a strong picture of this ancient world.

Excavations at Solnhofen

Mighty predator, *Allosaurus*

Dinosaur Anatomy

The illustrations in this book are based on specially made paeleontological models, made by experts in the field. This means that the illustrations show not just the body shape, but also skin texture, muscle formation and colourings.

4.6 BYA	3.5–2.8 BYA	1500–600 MYA	500–450 MYA	420 MYA	375 MYA
Formation of the Earth	First life on Earth – algae	First sea animals with shells and skeletons	First fish	First land animals – millipedes	First shark ancestors

Plant-eating
Triceratops

Carnivores and Herbivores, Land, Sea and Sky

The reptiles in this book are grouped together for ease of reference. First come the true dinosaurs: meat-eating 'carnivores' – including the ferocious *Tyrannosaurus rex*; and the vegetarian 'herbivores' – including sauropods with long, long necks. Following on, you will plunge into the watery depths with reptiles from the sea, then you will encounter the prehistoric beasts of the sky. Lastly, you will find an A–Z Dinosaur Fact File featuring 64 dinosaurs and their relatives. All their vital statistics are there, as well as a number of battles between the toughest of them.

Muscular tail Bipedal dinosaurs (those that walked on two legs) had strong, muscular tails.

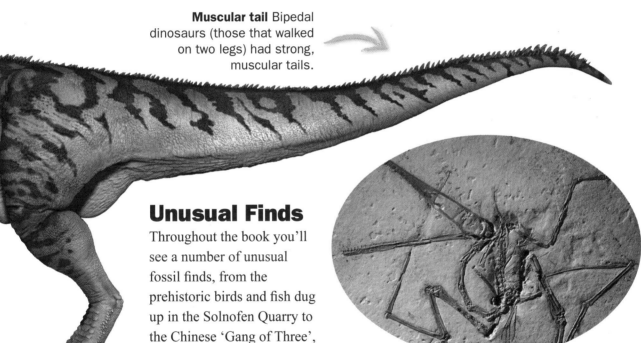

Unusual Finds

Throughout the book you'll see a number of unusual fossil finds, from the prehistoric birds and fish dug up in the Solnofen Quarry to the Chinese 'Gang of Three', the feathered dinosaurs that have caused so much debate.

Fossilized *Pterodactyl*

350–300 MYA	300–200 MYA	200–20 MYA	20–2 MYA	1.6–2 MYA	5–0 MYA
First amphibians and primitive insects	First reptiles, winged insects, primitive crocodiles and mammals. First dinosaurs!	Dinosaurs disappear and modern animal life begins to flourish	First chimpanzees and earliest humans	Mammoths disappear	First modern humans

Dinosaur Times

Dinosaurs, the most famous of all extinct animals, dominated Earth for about 160 million years. Reptiles evolved during the Carboniferous period, about 350 million years ago, and flourished during the succeeding Permian, Triassic, Jurassic and Cretaceous periods. During this Age of Reptiles, there were land-living reptiles, swimming reptiles, flying reptiles, herbivores, carnivores and omnivores – reptiles of all kinds in every environment. At the end of the Cretaceous era, about 65 million years ago, all the big reptiles died out and mammals took over. The Age of Reptiles was well under way before the first dinosaurs appeared around the end of the Triassic period, 225 million years ago.

Rauisuchian

Before the dinosaurs came along, the biggest of the hunters were a group of land-living crocodile relatives called rauisuchians. They had big heads and many sharp teeth and, although they were slow-moving, they were faster than the plant-eating reptiles that abounded at the time.

Scientists now know that dinosaurs lived millions of years ago and that there were many different types of these creatures roaming the land.

Rauisuchians were related to crocodiles, but were more upright. They had straight legs and walked rather than crawled.

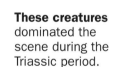

These creatures dominated the scene during the Triassic period.

Carboniferous	Permian	Triassic	Early/Mid Jurassic	Late Jurassic
360–286 MYA	286–248 MYA	245–208 MYA	208–157 MYA	157–146 MYA

An adult **Herrerasaurus** could reach lengths of **3 metres** (10 ft).

Tiger-sized

Herrerasaurus was a much bigger animal than *Eoraptor*, about the size of a tiger. One of the first dinosaurs, it was a primitive theropod, part of the group that includes all the meat-eaters.

Turn to page 178 to see what happens when three *Eoraptors* try to steal food from *Herrerasaurus*.

A speedy predator, *Eoraptor* was small, nimble and fierce.

Eoraptor

Eoraptor was about the size of a fox and, like all the dinosaurs to follow, walked on legs that were held straight under the body. This made it a much faster animal than the other reptiles that walked on legs sprawled out to the side. An *Eoraptor's* skull was made up of thin struts of bone, making it extremely light. The dinosaur's light bone structure enabled it to move fast. The skulls of most subsequent meat-eating dinosaurs were built like this.

Powerful Legs

This skeleton of a *Herrerasaurus* was found in Ishigualasto Provincial Park, Argentina, in South America. A meat-eating dinosaur, *Herrerasaurus* walked on strong hind legs, with its teeth and the claws on its arms held out to the front where they could do most damage. The back was held horizontally and the body was balanced by a long, muscular tail. This set the pattern for almost all meat-eating dinosaurs to come.

9

The First Known

Since civilization began, people have known about giant bones embedded in the rocks. They were spoken of in legends as the bones of mythical creatures. By the early 19th century, however, scientific knowledge had advanced sufficiently for scientists to begin to appreciate the true nature of fossils. In 1842, the British anatomist, Sir Richard Owen, invented the term 'dinosauria' (terrible lizards) to classify three fossil animals whose skeletons had been discovered in England during the previous two decades. One was the plant-eating *Iguanodon*, which is now quite well known. Another was the armoured *Hylaeosaurus*, which we still know very little about. The first of the trio to be brought to light and described, however, was the carnivorous *Megalosaurus*.

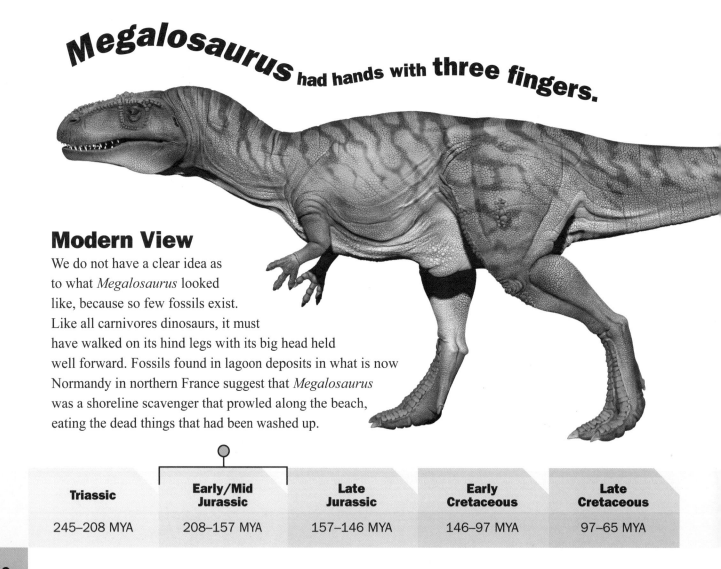

Megalosaurus had hands with **three fingers.**

Modern View

We do not have a clear idea as to what *Megalosaurus* looked like, because so few fossils exist. Like all carnivores dinosaurs, it must have walked on its hind legs with its big head held well forward. Fossils found in lagoon deposits in what is now Normandy in northern France suggest that *Megalosaurus* was a shoreline scavenger that prowled along the beach, eating the dead things that had been washed up.

Triassic	Early/Mid Jurassic	Late Jurassic	Early Cretaceous	Late Cretaceous
245–208 MYA	208–157 MYA	157–146 MYA	146–97 MYA	97–65 MYA

William Buckland (1784–1856)

This 19th-century clergyman was typical of his time. When away from his pulpit he spent his spare time carrying out all kinds of scientific research. Most of the fossils he studied were those of sea-living animals – seashells and marine reptiles. Fossils of land-living animals have always been harder to find. Buckland may not have invented the name *Megalosaurus* but he was the scholar who completed all the scientific work on it.

The first *Megalosaurus* jaw was unearthed in Oxfordshire, England, in about 1815.

Megalosaurus Jaw

The lower jawbone and teeth of *Megalosaurus* were the first parts of the animal to be discovered. William Buckland studied them and deduced from the sharp pointed teeth that they had belonged to a carnivore, and that it had been a large reptile. Other scientists studied the remains in the 1820s and one of them came up with the name *Megalosaurus*.

For some time, the name *Megalosaurus* was applied to the fossil of any meat-eating dinosaur found in Europe.

First Dinosaur Theme Park

Because of the great public interest in science in the mid-19th century, part of Crystal Palace park in South London was developed as an ancient landscape. Statues (which still stand today) were erected showing the three dinosaurs and the marine reptiles that were known at the time. All that was known of *Megalosaurus* was its jawbone, teeth and a few fragments of bone. Since nobody knew what the animal actually looked like, it was modelled as a fearsome four-footed dragon-like creature.

11

All About Fossils

Our knowledge of dinosaurs comes from the fossils we find in sedimentary rocks (rocks formed from sand and mud). Sedimentary rocks are often layered. The layers are called 'beds' or 'strata', and they usually occur in sequences, with the oldest at the bottom and the most recently made at the top. Fossils found in the layers reveal when and where different creatures lived on Earth. Because the fossils are simply bones that have turned to stone, they also help scientists to work out what the different creatures looked like when they were alive. When scientists find a new dinosaur, they give it a Latin name: *Tyrannosaurus rex* means 'king of the tyrant lizards' in Latin.

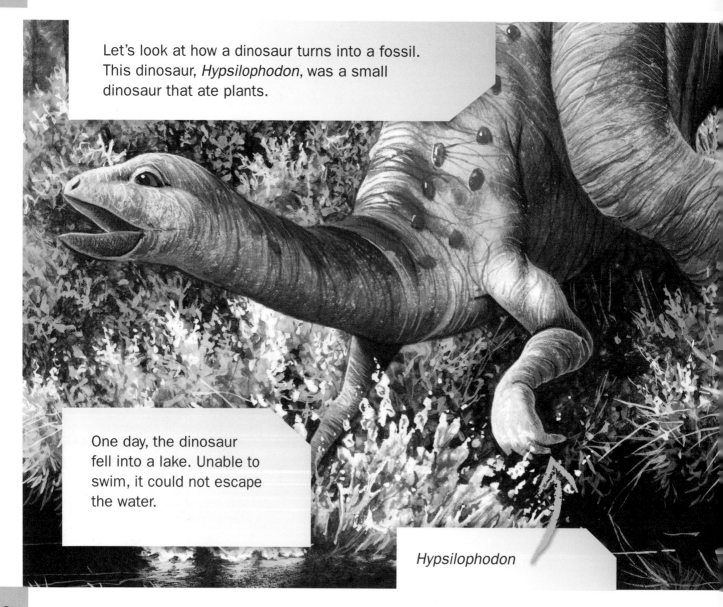

Let's look at how a dinosaur turns into a fossil. This dinosaur, *Hypsilophodon*, was a small dinosaur that ate plants.

One day, the dinosaur fell into a lake. Unable to swim, it could not escape the water.

Hypsilophodon

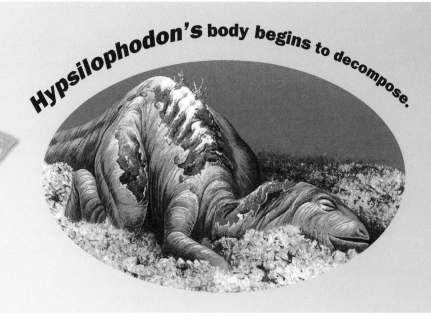

Hypsilophodon's body begins to decompose.

The *Hypsilophodon* drowned and its body fell to the bottom of the lake. Other animals in the lake ate the *Hypsilophodon's* skin.

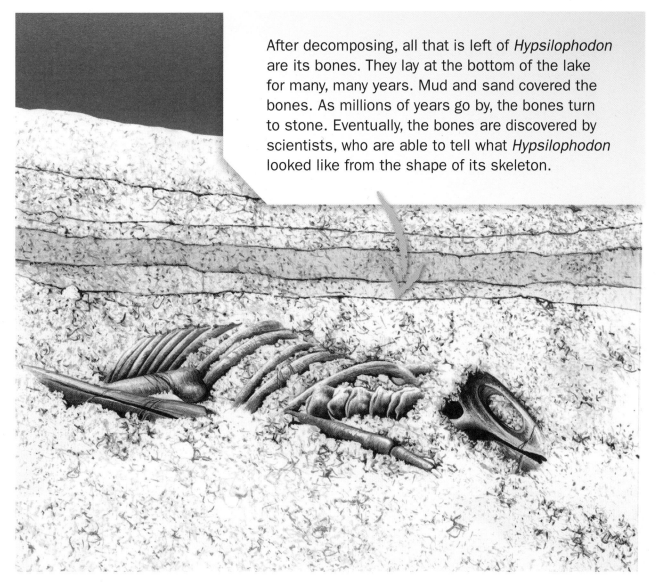

After decomposing, all that is left of *Hypsilophodon* are its bones. They lay at the bottom of the lake for many, many years. Mud and sand covered the bones. As millions of years go by, the bones turn to stone. Eventually, the bones are discovered by scientists, who are able to tell what *Hypsilophodon* looked like from the shape of its skeleton.

At 15 m (50 ft) long, **carcharodontosaurus** was a true giant.

Chapter 1:
Carnivores

Which dinosaur had the **strongest jaws?** What is the name of the **fastest** dinosaur on two legs? Just how big was the **largest** of the carnivores? And what was planet Earth like all those **millions of years** ago? You'll find the answers to these, and many more questions, in this chapter on the **mighty meat-eaters** of the Reptile Age. **Discover** how the most **fearsome** beasts of all time roamed the land, terrorizing their prey, sometimes hunting creatures down in packs. **Find out** which of them fed on the leftovers of another dinosaur's kill, shredding the flesh with their **razor-sharp teeth.** And learn how and where scientists discovered the **fossils** that have helped to tell the story so far.

Early Hunters

Most of the early meat-eating dinosaurs were small animals, some of them no bigger than modern-day domestic cats and dogs. They probably fed mainly on even smaller animals, such as lizards and the early mammals. However, most of the plant-eating reptiles of the time were quite large animals and would also have made good prey for the meat-eaters. Some of the earliest dinosaurs adopted a strategy of hunting in packs so that they could bring down and kill some of these big plant-eaters. Today, such teamwork is still used in the wild by animals such as Canadian wolves, which hunt moose much bigger than themselves. Similarly, on the African plains, groups of hyenas attack wildebeest that are far bigger than they are.

Coelophysis

Late Triassic *Coelophysis* was a 3-metre (10-ft) long carnivore. In the 1940s, a whole group of them was discovered fossilized in New Mexico, evidently having perished in a drought. Since they had both lived and died together, it was deduced that these animals moved about in packs or family groups. Another behavioural trait came to light when the skeleton of a youngster was found in the stomach area of one of the adults. Perhaps they had been so desperate for food that they ate their own kind.

Three-toed trackways found in the Appalachian Mountains, USA, are thought to be those of *Coelophysis*.

Triassic	Early/Mid Jurassic	Late Jurassic	Early Cretaceous	Late Cretaceous
245–208 MYA	208–157 MYA	157–146 MYA	146–97 MYA	97–65 MYA

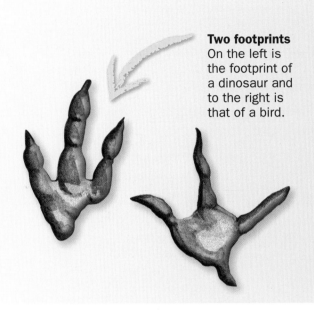

Two footprints
On the left is the footprint of a dinosaur and to the right is that of a bird.

Bird & Dinosaur Footprints

Birds and dinosaurs are so closely related it is little wonder the footprints of one could be mistaken for those of the other. In a series of ridges of Jurassic and Cretaceous rocks in the flanks of the Rocky Mountains west of Denver, USA, there are fossilized footprints of both dinosaurs and birds. Bird footprints can be distinguished from dinosaur prints by the greater spread of their toes – about 90° as opposed to about 45°. There is also often a trace of the little fourth toe pointing backwards. In dinosaurs, this toe is usually well clear of the ground.

Syntarsus

In 1972, a remarkable deposit of fossils was found in Rhodesia (now Zimbabwe). A mass of bones lay in fine river sediment, sandwiched between rocks formed from sand dunes. The fossils were of a pack of small meat-eating dinosaurs of different sizes and ages. They seemed to have drowned in a flash flood that struck as they were crossing a dry river bed. These meat-eating dinosaurs, named *Syntarsus*, were almost identical in build to *Coelophysis* and some scientists think they are likely to have been a species of the same animal.

Some scientists believe that *Syntarsus* might have had feathers.

One World

In late Triassic and early Jurassic times the world was very different from the way it is today. All the continental landmasses were joined together in one area, called Pangaea. Since there was only one landmass, animals of the same kind were able to migrate everywhere. This is why we find the remains of almost identical animals in New Mexico and Connecticut, USA, as well as in Zimbabwe, thousands of miles away on the African continent.

The supercontinent of ancient times.

Triassic World

By the time of the Triassic period – 245–208 million years ago – all the landmasses had come together as a single, vast supercontinent that we call Panagea. One huge ocean, called Panthalassa, covered the rest of the world. Because Panagea was so vast, most of it was a long way from the cooling sea. At the centre of the giant supercontinent was an intensely hot and uninhabitable desert. All life existed in the temperate coastal areas.

Triassic means three-fold. Geologists working in Germany in 1834 noticed three types of rocks from this time and named the period after their discovery.

The Triassic world was inhabited by **early hunters,** like *Coelophysis*.

In the forest areas, vegetation included **tree ferns, conifers and horsetails.**

The **single supercontinent** was a solid landmass so animals could easily migrate from one habitable area to another one. Fossils of the same animal have been found as far apart as South Africa and Germany.

Crest-headed Beasts

Look at the bright colours of many birds – the long tail feathers of a peacock, the gaudy bill of a toucan, the red breast of a robin. Colour is part of a bird's method of communication. Their brains can 'read' the colours they see, enabling them to recognize whether another bird is a friend or foe. Birds are related to dinosaurs, which had similar brains and senses. It is very likely that dinosaurs also used colour for communication. Some dinosaurs (especially among the carnivores) had crests and horns as brightly coloured as the plumage of modern birds.

Dilophosaurus means 'double-crested lizard'.

Dilophosaurus in Life

In life, *Dilophosaurus* probably looked dazzling. It seems very likely that its two parallel crests were particularly colourful either to frighten rivals or attract a mate from far away. It is also possible that the males had larger crests than the females, for the same reasons. The rest of the animal may also have been brightly coloured to back up the signals given by the crests. Dewlaps (flaps of skin beneath the chin) may have been brightly coloured like modern lizards, and would also have been part of the display.

Triassic	Early/Mid Jurassic	Late Jurassic	Early Cretaceous	Late Cretaceous
245–208 MYA	208–157 MYA	157–146 MYA	146–97 MYA	97–65 MYA

Horned Monster

One of the fiercest dinosaurs of the late Jurassic was *Ceratosaurus*, which lived in North America and Tanzania in East Africa. It had a heavy head with a horn on the nose and another pair of horns above the eyes. The heavy skull suggests it may have fought with rivals by head-battering, but the horns were very lightly built and would not have been much use as weapons. They may have been used only for display.

Monolophosaurus

The crest of *Monolophosaurus*, a medium-sized middle Jurassic meat-eating dinosaur from China, was made up of a pair of skull bones fused together and growing upwards. Air gaps and channels between these bones were connected to the nostrils and may have been used to amplify grunts generated in the animal's throat. In this way the crest would have helped it communicate by sound as well as visually.

Dilophosaurus Skeleton

Dilophosaurus was a bear-sized, meat-eating dinosaur from the early Jurassic of North America. The first skeleton found had semicircular plate-like structures lying near it. Later finds showed that these structures were crests that ran parallel to one another along the length of the skull.

No skeleton can ever tell us what colour dinosaur crests were in real life.

Forward Thinking

The early Jurassic meat-eater from Antarctica, *Cryolophosaurus*, had a crest that curled up and forwards above its eyes. The bony core was probably covered in brightly-coloured horn or skin. *Cryolophosaurus* is the only dinosaur known to have had a crest that ran across the skull rather than along it. At 8 metres (26 ft) long, it was probably the biggest meat-eater of its time, its size enhanced still further by the crest.

Spinosaurids – the Fish Eaters

We normally think of fish-eating animals as creatures that live in the water. However, there are many land-living animals that like to take fish too. Grizzly bears are often seen beside waterfalls hooking out migrating salmon as they leap up to their spawning grounds, and otters live mostly on land but hunt fish. It was the same in the Jurassic period. One particular family of land-dwelling dinosaurs – the spinosaurids – seem to have been particularly well-equipped for fishing. They had long jaws with many small teeth, and a big claw on each hand.

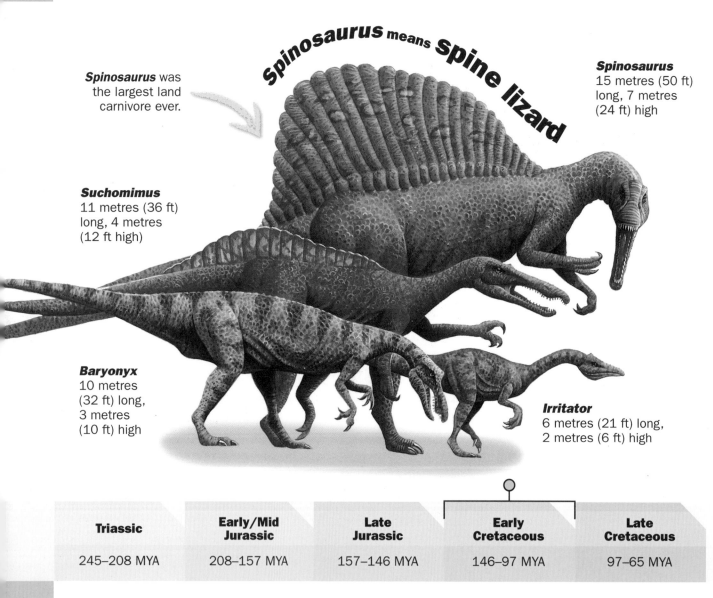

Spinosaurus means **Spine lizard**

Spinosaurus was the largest land carnivore ever.

Spinosaurus
15 metres (50 ft) long, 7 metres (24 ft) high

Suchomimus
11 metres (36 ft) long, 4 metres (12 ft high)

Baryonyx
10 metres (32 ft) long, 3 metres (10 ft) high

Irritator
6 metres (21 ft) long, 2 metres (6 ft) high

Triassic	Early/Mid Jurassic	Late Jurassic	Early Cretaceous	Late Cretaceous
245–208 MYA	208–157 MYA	157–146 MYA	146–97 MYA	97–65 MYA

Menacing Mimic

Suchomimus was found in a remote dune-covered area of the Sahara in 1998. An enormous predatory dinosaur with a skull like a crocodile's and huge thumb claws, it measured 11 metres (36 ft) in length and 4 metres (12 ft) high at the hip. The thumb claws and powerfully built forelimbs were used to snare prey, and the thin sail along its back – which reached a height of 50 centimetres (2 ft) over the hips – may have been brightly coloured for display.

Each tooth is designed to bury deep into the prey's flesh.

The spinosaurids lived in early Cretaceous times, and their remains have been found across the world, from Southern England to North Africa and South America.

Big Bite

Many modern reptiles have similarities to the spinosaurids. Crocodiles and alligators, for example, have long jaws and many teeth – just like the *Spinosaurus* tooth above – and hunt for fish in a similar way.

Heavy Claw

Baryonyx was discovered by an amateur fossil collector in southern England in 1983. The skeleton was so complete that it gave us the first clear view of what these animals looked like. *Baryonyx* was an unusual meat-eating dinosaur that had crocodile-like jaws packed with sharp teeth, and long forelimbs with hooked claws, which were used to catch fish. *Baryonyx* stood 3 metres (10 ft) tall, and each of its claws measured nearly 35 centimetres (12 in) long. It probably ranged over a large area stretching from England to North Africa.

Spiny Customer

Spinosaurus was excavated in Egypt in 1915. Unfortunately, its remains were destroyed when its museum in Germany was bombed in World War II. What we do know about it was that it was bigger than *Tyrannosaurus* and had a fin down its back, almost 2 metres (6.5 ft) tall. The fin was probably used to cool the animal in hot weather. In 1999, an American expedition found its original quarry in Egypt, so there may be hope of finding new specimens in the future.

The Smallest Dinosaurs

When we think about dinosaurs (terrible lizards), we usually visualize huge and fierce animals. However, some dinosaurs were actually quite small beasts not much bigger than chickens. Scuttling about the ground among the giants, small dinosaurs were probably more common than the big ones. Unfortunately, as their bones were so lightweight and their skeletons quite delicate, very few have been preserved as fossils. Nevertheless, a number of good specimens have been found and some of these were preserved in great detail.

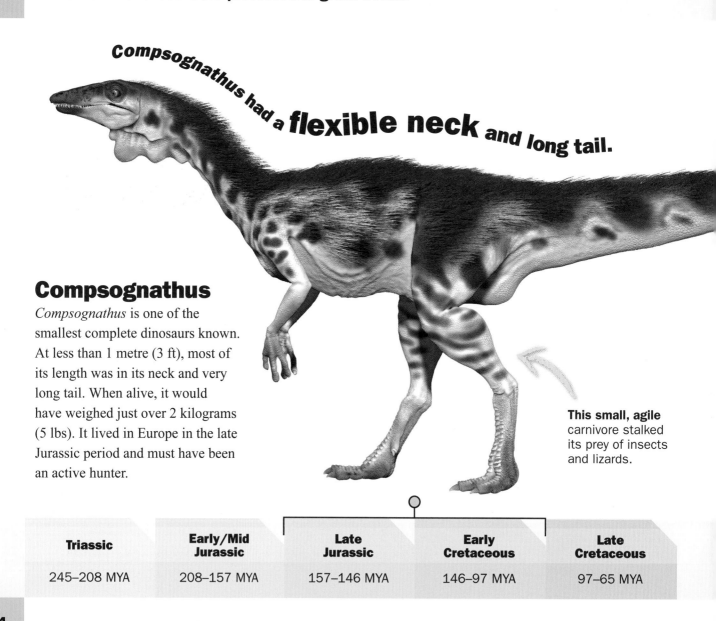

Compsognathus had a **flexible neck** *and long tail.*

Compsognathus

Compsognathus is one of the smallest complete dinosaurs known. At less than 1 metre (3 ft), most of its length was in its neck and very long tail. When alive, it would have weighed just over 2 kilograms (5 lbs). It lived in Europe in the late Jurassic period and must have been an active hunter.

This small, agile carnivore stalked its prey of insects and lizards.

Triassic	Early/Mid Jurassic	Late Jurassic	Early Cretaceous	Late Cretaceous
245–208 MYA	208–157 MYA	157–146 MYA	146–97 MYA	97–65 MYA

Tiniest Footprint

In the 1970s, the tiny footprint of a dinosaur that could have been no bigger than a thrush was found in the late Triassic rocks of Newfoundland in Canada. The arrangement of the toes is typical of the meat-eating dinosaurs of the Triassic. The print is the only trace we have of the smallest dinosaur ever found. Whether it was a youngster or fully grown, nobody yet knows.

Turn to page 166 for a grizzly standoff between *Compsognathus* and its near relative, *Archeopteryx*.

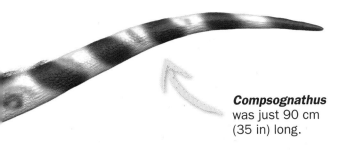

Compsognathus was just 90 cm (35 in) long.

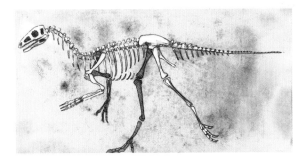

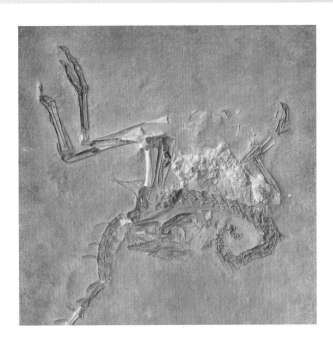

Nqwebasaurus

Scientists became very excited in the late 1990s when they found the almost complete skeleton of 1-metre (3-ft) long *Nqwebasaurus* embedded in early Cretaceous rocks in South Africa. It proved that the family to which most of the small meat-eating dinosaurs belonged (the coelurosaurids) had existed in the southern continents during the Cretaceous period, as well as in North America, Europe and Asia.

Compsognathus Skeleton

Two *Compsognathus* skeletons have been found: one in France, the other in Germany. The German specimen was particularly well-preserved in fine limestone. Not only is the skeleton clearly visible, but also the contents of its stomach, showing that its last meal included a small lizard. Some scientists thought *Compsognathus* was the baby of some other type of dinosaur but blobs scattered around the German skeleton are probably eggs, as yet unlaid when the animal died. They prove the German *Compsognathus* was an adult female.

Jurassic Giant

Some dinosaurs really did live up to their reputation of being enormous fearsome beasts. Probably the most terrifying animal of the late Jurassic period was *Allosaurus*. Its remains have been found in both Tanzania, Africa, and in the sequence of rocks known as the Morrison Formation, which stretches down the western United States from the Canadian border to New Mexico. These deposits yielded the most important dinosaur discoveries made in the second half of the 19th century. Over a hundred different kinds of dinosaur (mostly plant-eaters) were found there. The most powerful of the meat-eaters found was *Allosaurus*.

All Muscle

By studying the arrangement of bones in the skeleton, scientists have worked out what the fleshed-up *Allosaurus* would have looked like. The leg muscles would have allowed it to move at speeds of up to 30 km/h (18 mph) – not particularly swift, but fast enough to catch the slow-moving herbivores of the time.

Allosaurus's hands had three claws: one claw, at 25 centimetres (10 in) long, was much larger than the other two. The joint on this first finger allowed the huge claw to turn inwards. *Allosaurus* would have been able to grasp its prey, kill it, then rip it apart. The span of its hand would have been wide enough to grasp the head of an adult man, had there been such a person around in Jurassic times!

Triassic	Early/Mid Jurassic	Late Jurassic	Early Cretaceous	Late Cretaceous
245–208 MYA	208–157 MYA	157–146 MYA	146–97 MYA	97–65 MYA

Hunting

The bones of plant-eaters such as *Camarasaurus* are found throughout the Morrison Formation, often mixed up with the broken teeth of meat-eating dinosaurs. Discoveries like these suggest that the big plant-eaters – especially sick ones – were often attacked and killed by big meat-eaters like *Allosaurus*. Once the killer had eaten its fill, packs of smaller meat-eaters, such as *Ceratosaurus*, may have scavenged what was left.

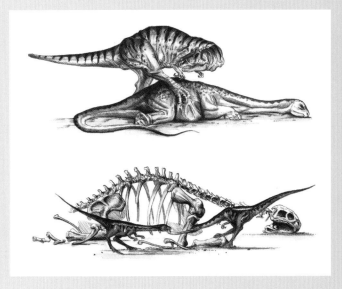

Allosaurus would have needed massive neck muscles to move its enormous head.

Skull

A typical *Allosaurus* skull was about 1 metre (3.5 ft) long. The jaws were armed with more than 70 teeth, some measuring 8 centimetres (3 inches). The teeth were curved, pointed and serrated, ideal for ripping the flesh of large plant-eating dinosaurs. Joints between the skull bones allowed the snout to move up and down to help manipulate food. The lower jaws were hinged so they could expand sideways to allow the animal to gulp down big chunks of meat.

Big Feet

The feet of *Allosaurus* had three powerful toes, muscular enough to carry the entire weight of the adult, which might have been as much as 5,000 kilograms (11,000 lbs). The toes were not equipped with hooked claws, but with broad hooves that would have helped to bear the great weight.

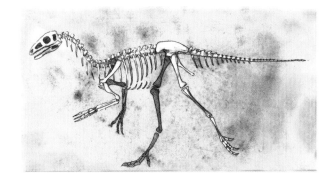

Allosaurus in Life

We have a fairly good idea what *Allosaurus* looked like from the thousands of bone specimens (some almost complete skeletons) that have been found. These bones belonged to juveniles that measured about 3 metres (10 ft) from nose to tail-tip, and to adults of about 9 metres (30 ft) long. Some of the *Allosaurus* bones found must have come from 12-metre (40-ft) monsters. Mounted casts of *Allosaurus* skeletons can be seen in many museums around the world. The actual bones are usually kept behind the scenes for research.

Fast Hunters

Back in the late 19th/early 20th centuries there was a popular theory that modern birds and dinosaurs were related. This theory fell out of favour for a long time but was revived in the 1960s when a group of dinosaurs, extremely bird-like in their build, were discovered. They ranged from the size of a goose to the size of a tiger and had wing-like joints in their forearms. They also had strong hind legs with huge, sickle-like killing claws on their feet, showing that they were very fast runners and fierce hunters. These dinosaurs are known as the dromaeosaurids (part of a larger group called the maniraptorans) and are commonly referred to as the 'raptors'.

A Range of Dromaeosaurids

About the size of a goose, *Bambiraptor* is the smallest of the dromaeosaurids. Turkey-sized *Velociraptor* is probably the best-known. Scientists were first alerted to the bird-like nature of these animals in the 1960s, when tiger-sized *Deinonychus* was discovered. Bigger dromaeosaurids are known but only from bone fragments. *Utahraptor* probably weighed more than a tonne while *Megaraptor* (not shown), known only from a super-long killing claw, must have approached the size of the big meat-eaters, such as *Allosaurus*. Apart from the Argentinian *Megaraptor*, all these animals were found in late Cretaceous rocks in North America.

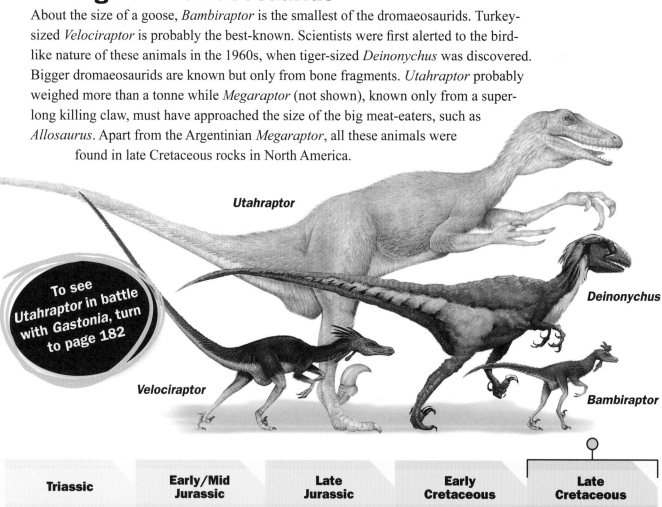

Utahraptor

To see Utahraptor in battle with Gastonia, turn to page 182

Deinonychus

Velociraptor

Bambiraptor

Triassic	Early/Mid Jurassic	Late Jurassic	Early Cretaceous	Late Cretaceous
245–208 MYA	208–157 MYA	157–146 MYA	146–97 MYA	97–65 MYA

Terrible Claws

The skeleton of a plant-eating *Tenontosaurus*, found in late Cretaceous rocks in Montana, USA, was surrounded by the remains of several *Deinonychus*. This suggests that *Deinonychus* hunted in packs, surrounded a prey animal and then slashed it to death. With its big brain and balancing tail, a *Deinonychus* could have stood on one foot and slashed with the other, or it may have hung on to its prey with its clawed hands and slashed away with both hind feet, as cats do. Before it died, this *Tenontosaurus* must have put up a fight and killed some of its attackers.

Deinonychus had strong muscles for running and jumping.

Rahonavis had a raised sickle claw on its second toe.

Bird or Dromaeosaurid?

Right down to the killing claw on its foot *Rahonavis*, an early Cretaceous bird from Madagascar, had the skeleton of a dromaeosaurid. If it had not been for the functional wings, it would have been grouped with the dromaeosaurids.

Early Bird

This fossil of the first bird, *Archaeopteryx*, dating from the late Jurassic period, was found in Germany in 1877. If it had not been for the feather impressions in the fossil, the skeleton would have been mistaken for that of a dinosaur because it has a toothed jaw, clawed hands and a long tail. As well as evolving into modern birds, it is possible that some of *Archaeopteryx's* descendants lost their powers of flight and developed into the dromaeosaurids and other related meat-eating dinosaurs of the Cretaceous period. They were certainly closely related to one another.

Eggs & Nests

Some dinosaurs built nests and laid eggs. The first known dinosaur nests were found by an expedition sent to the Gobi desert from the American Museum of Natural History in 1923. The nests were among remains of herds of the horned dinosaur *Protoceratops*. Alongside the supposed *Protoceratops* eggs lay the skeleton of a toothless meat-eater *Oviraptor*. This so-called 'egg thief' was thought to have been buried in a sandstorm while digging up the eggs. But, as sometimes happens, more evidence caused later palaeontologists to re-evaluate this interpretation. In the 1990s, another expedition to the Gobi desert found the fossil of an *Oviraptor* sitting on a nest, incubating eggs, which meant those first nests must also have been *Oviraptor* nests!

Nesting Dinosaur

In the 1990s, a fossil was found of an *Oviraptor* sitting on a nest with its arms spread protectively around some eggs, evidently keeping them warm with the heat of its body. Modern birds do this efficiently as their feathers provide excellent insulation. This is one of the indirect lines of evidence that suggests that *Oviraptor*, and many other bird-like dinosaurs, had feathers.

Oviraptor

With its long fingers, just right for grasping eggs, *Oviraptor* may after all have been an egg-eating dinosaur. Certainly, its head suggests it could have been. Its very short, beak-like mouth and its gullet, situated right over the widest part of its jaw, were ideal for swallowing something big and round. As in modern egg-eating snakes, two bones protruding down from its palate were perfectly positioned to tear open an egg on its way down. There seems to have been little else for it to eat on the desert plains of late Cretaceous Mongolia.

Some dinosaurs built nests and laid eggs, just like modern-day birds do.

Triassic	Early/Mid Jurassic	Late Jurassic	Early Cretaceous	Late Cretaceous
245–208 MYA	208–157 MYA	157–146 MYA	146–97 MYA	97–65 MYA

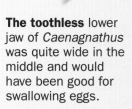

The toothless lower jaw of *Caenagnathus* was quite wide in the middle and would have been good for swallowing eggs.

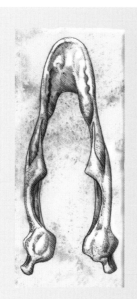

Caenagnathus Jawbone

Caenagnathus was a dinosaur that probably resembled *Oviraptor*, and may have been an egg eater. So far only its jaw has been found, so *Caenagnathus* remains a bit of a mystery. The jaw of *Caenagnathus* was similar to that of *Chirostenotes*. This was a turkey-sized dinosaur with very long fingers that would have enabled it to raid other dinosaur nests for their eggs. Perhaps there were many different kinds of egg-stealing dinosaurs in late Cretaceous times.

Troodon had large forward-facing eyes.

Scientists think that *Troodon* had long feathers on its arms and tail.

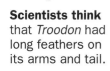

Troodon

Troodon was one of the maniraptorans, but was not quite as bird-like as the dromaeosaurids. This small meat-eater of the late Cretaceous period was about 2.5 metres (8 ft) long. Fossils of *Troodon* nests show that there were oval ridges of mud surrounding the eggs, very much like the nests of *Oviraptor*. The eggs were laid in pairs, which suggests that this dinosaur had a pair of oviducts (egg tubes) within its body. Modern birds have just one.

Leafy Nests

Big, heavy dinosaurs did not sit on their eggs – they might break them. Instead, they hid them in piles of leaves to keep safe and warm.

Bird or Dinosaur?

As well as finding the first dinosaur nests, the American expeditions to the Gobi desert in the 1920s uncovered many other dinosaur remains. One of these we now call *Mononykus* was a total puzzle. Was it a bird or was it a dinosaur? If it was a bird, its arms were too short for it to fly. If it was a dinosaur, what good were hands reduced to a single finger with a big claw? In the 1980s, when new specimens were found, *Mononykus* was found to have belonged to a group of related animals, the alvarezsaurids – a distinct group within the maniraptorans – that ranged from South America to Central Asia. Today, we still do not know whether they were birds or dinosaurs.

Alvarezsaurids

The first alvarezsaurid to be described was *Alvarezsaurus* itself, found in Argentina in the 1970s. This specimen had no forelimbs, so did not look too unusual, but it did have a very bird-like body. In the early 1990s, good specimens of *Mononykus* were found in Mongolia and scientists realized these were two very similar animals. In 1991, again in Argentina, the discovery of *Patagonykus* confirmed there were several related animals in the alvarezsaurid group.

Mononykus looked like a very lightly-built, meat-eating dinosaur with spindly legs and a long tail. The two forelimbs are remarkable. They are very short in length and have a shelf of bone, which in modern birds would support wing feathers, and each bears a single stout, stubby claw. These forelimbs probably evolved from the functional wings of a flying ancestor, such as the late Jurassic *Archaeopteryx*.

Mononykus had unusually short forelimbs.

Mononykus is the best known and most complete of the alvarezsaurids.

Triassic	Early/Mid Jurassic	Late Jurassic	Early Cretaceous	Late Cretaceous
245–208 MYA	208–157 MYA	157–146 MYA	146–97 MYA	97–65 MYA

A Halfway Stage

All sorts of other animals seem to have been intermediate in the evolution from dinosaurs to birds. At the size of an ostrich, *Unenlagia* was far too big to fly, even though its arms were in the form of small wings. Perhaps these wings helped the animal balance and provided direction control as it ran across open plains at speed. Whatever their function, they probably evolved from the working wings of an ancestor that did fly.

One function of non-flying wings in modern running birds is for display.

Flightless rheas are native to South America.

Showy Wings

The ostrich makes a big show of its wing feathers when it is courting a mate or threatening an enemy. It is quite possible that the part-bird/part-dinosaur animals of the Cretaceous period also had flamboyant feathers on their flightless wings and used them for display. Unfortunately, such behaviour cannot be proven by fossil evidence.

Running Rhea

The modern, flightless rhea is the running bird of today's dusty Argentinian plains. It uses its stumpy wings to steer itself while running. Today's flightless birds have evolved from flying ancestors, just as the maniraptorans probably did back in the age of dinosaurs.

Bird Mimics

One group of dinosaurs has always been thought to look very much like birds. Ornithomimids (bird mimics) had plump, compact bodies; big eyes; toothless beaks on small heads that were supported on long, slender necks, and long running legs with thick muscles close to the hip. Typical of the group was a dinosaur called *Struthiomimus* (ostrich mimic) from the late Cretaceous period. Although they fall into the category of meat-eating dinosaurs and would have descended from purely carnivorous ancestors, these dinosaurs were probably omnivorous, eating fruit and leaves as well as insects and small vertebrates, such as lizards. Ostriches and other ground birds of today are also omnivores.

Ornithomimids

All ornithomimids looked similar but varied somewhat in size. *Struthiomimus* was about the size of an ostrich. *Pelecanimimus* had a pouch of skin beneath its long jaws, which had hundreds of tiny teeth in them. This suggests the teeth of the group became smaller and smaller before disappearing altogether in the later ornithomimids. *Garudimimus*, named after a mythical Hindu bird, had a small crest on its head. The biggest known was *Gallimimus*, the 'chicken mimic', at 4–5 metres (13–16 ft) long.

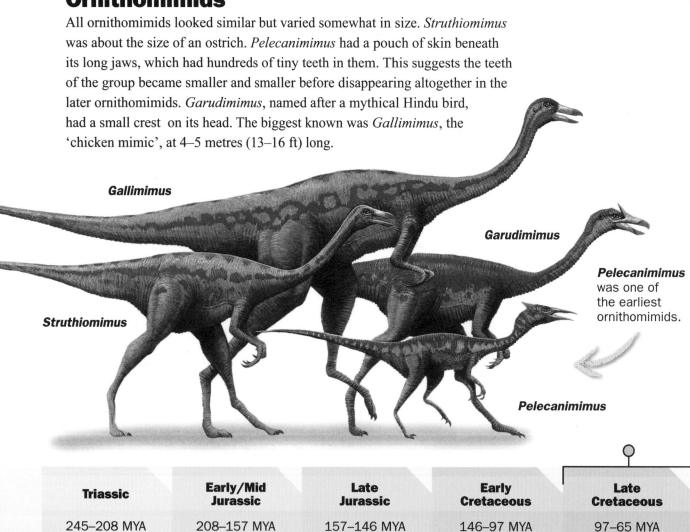

Gallimimus

Garudimimus

Pelecanimimus
was one of
the earliest
ornithomimids.

Struthiomimus

Pelecanimimus

Triassic	Early/Mid Jurassic	Late Jurassic	Early Cretaceous	Late Cretaceous
245–208 MYA	208–157 MYA	157–146 MYA	146–97 MYA	97–65 MYA

34

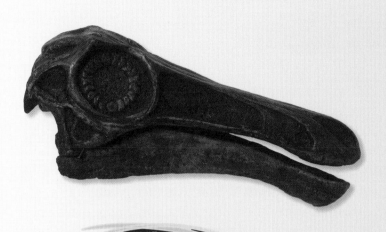

Gallimimus Skeleton

Gallimimus is probably the best known of the Ornithomimids. It had a small toothless beak, which it used for cropping fruit and vegetation. This dinosaur was built for speed, and could run at up to 80 km/h (50 mph), as fast as a race horse. It usually paced around slowly, stalking small mammals or snapping up seeds and insects, but its speed meant that it could escape from most predators. Its long tail acted as a counterbalance to the front of the body, propelling it forward while it sprinted. Its hipbone also pointed forward.

This skeleton is mounted on display at the Royal Tyrrell Museum of Paleontology, Drumheller, Alberta, Canada.

Built For Speed

As with most meat-eating dinosaurs the skeleton of an ornithomimid, such as this *Ornithomimus*, is very bird-like. Its head would have been held farther forward than that of an ostrich, balanced by its long tail. However, they had very similar legs with a very short thighbone that would have held all the muscles so that the lower leg and the toes were worked only by tendons. This gives a very lightweight leg that could move quickly – a running leg.

Emu

A modern emu is a typical plains-living animal. The keen eyes in the head, held high on the top of a long neck, are able to spot danger coming from a long way away across the open spaces. The strong running legs are then able to take the bird out of danger at great speed. Because of the physical similarity, we think that the ornithomimids of the late Cretaceous period had a similar lifestyle on the open plains of North America and central Asia.

Ornithomimus had some ostrich-like features.

Segnosaurids

Sometimes, part of a skeleton is so unlike any known dinosaur, nobody knows what kind it is. Such is the case with segnosaurids. In the 1920s, the first bones, found in late Cretaceous rocks in Mongolia, were thought to be from a giant turtle, but were re-classified as dinosaur remains in the 1970s. The various bits of bone were all so unalike they seemed to be from different families of dinosaur. Even now, the name therizinosaurid is sometimes used for the group; the name was first used as the original classification of the forelimb, as opposed to segnosaurid, the name set up when the skull and backbone were studied. These dinosaurs were thought to be meat-eaters; then prosauropods, one of the long-necked plant-eaters. They are back with the meat-eaters for the time being.

Segnosaurus

Typical of the group, *Segnosaurus* had a relatively small head, and a heavy body supported on short hind legs. Its curved backbone must have given it a stooped appearance. Perhaps its most surprising feature is the presence of enormous sickle-like talons on its hands. One segnosaurid, *Beipiaosaurus* (discovered in 1999), had the remains of fine feather-like structures around its limbs. At 6 metres (20 ft) long, it is the biggest known feathered dinosaur. Like some of the more bird-like dinosaurs, Segnosaurids seem to have been covered in some kind of plumage.

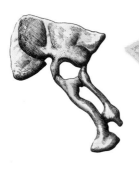

Segnosaurus's hipbone adds confusion to its classification.

Segnosaurus Hipbone

The hipbones of meat-eating dinosaurs are usually quite distinctive. The pubis bone at the front points forwards. In the segnosaurids, the pubis bone sweeps backwards. This is usually only seen in plant-eating dinosaurs, as it gives more space for the big plant-eating guts that such animals need. It would have given the body of this dinosaur a very dumpy appearance. This is part of what makes the whole group a puzzle.

Triassic	Early/Mid Jurassic	Late Jurassic	Early Cretaceous	Late Cretaceous
245–208 MYA	208–157 MYA	157–146 MYA	146–97 MYA	97–65 MYA

Erlikosaurus's **skull** shares similarities with that of some big plant-eating dinosaurs.

Erlikosaurus Skull

The best known segnosaurid skull is that of *Erlikosaurus*. Behind its toothless beak the teeth are small and leaf-shaped. Some scientists have suggested this might be the skull of a fish-eating dinosaur and that the foot bones (which are also unusual) could have been webbed for swimming. However, the rest of the skeleton suggests that it could not have been a swimming animal, but rather one that lived on land.

A Modern Parallel

The anteater is a modern animal with claws that seem too big for its body. It uses them to rip through the tough walls of anthills to get at the living chambers of the ant colony. Some scientists have suggested that this is how the segnosaurids lived, while other scientists doubt that this diet could have supported such a big animal.

There are various species of anteater, all native to Central and South America.

Mighty Claws

The forearms of *Therizinosaurus* were almost as long as those of the mysterious *Deinocheirus*. However, much of their length consisted of the fingers, one of which had a claw that measured 70 centimetres (2.5 ft) long. That was just the length of the bone of the claw. With the horny sheath on it, the claw would have been half as long again. What could this claw have been used for? Palaeontologists are still guessing today.

19th-century Dinosaur Discoveries

Pachypodes!

1825 Gideon Mantell names *Iguanodon*.

1832 German palaeontologist Hermann von Meyer names the animals found by Buckland and Mantell '*pachypodes*'. The classification is not used.

1824 William Buckland names *Megalosaurus*.

1898 Barnum Brown finds the first *Tyrannosaurus* remains.

1877–97 American palaeontologists Othniel Charles Marsh and Edward Drinker compete to discover new dinosaurs. Known as the 'Bone Wars' about 160 new dinosaurs are found by the end of the century.

1878 The discovery of a herd of *Iguanodon* in a mine in Belgium gives the first clear idea of what a whole dinosaur looked like.

1837 Von Meyer finds the first prosauropod, *Plateosaurus*.

Dinosauria!

1833 The first armoured dinosaur ever to be found is named *Hylaeosaurus* by Mantell.

1842 Sir Richard Owen comes up with the name '*Dinosauria*' to describe the animals known at this time. Unlike Meyer's suggestion, the name proves popular.

The 19th century saw great scientific developments in the study of dinosaur remains. Because of this, a picture of dinosaurs as a group of actual living animals emerged.

1859 Charles Darwin publishes *On the Origin of Species*.

1858 American anatomist Joseph Leidy finds the duckbill dinosaur *Hadrosaurus*.

1853 The first dinosaur theme park opens in England in the grounds of Crystal Palace, south London.

1855 The first dinosaurs are found in North America.

Tyrannosaurids

At 12 metres (39 ft) long and 6 metres (20 ft) tall, *Tyrannosaurus* must have been the scourge of the North American continent at the end of the dinosaur age. So far, about 15 specimens of *Tyrannosaurus* have been discovered in various states of completeness. From these we have built up a picture of what the mighty beasts looked like. However, there is still much debate about how they lived. Some scientists think they actively hunted, perhaps waiting in ambush for duckbills, the big plant-eaters of the time, then charging out at them from the cover of the forest. Others insist they were too big for such activity but would have scavenged carrion, the meat of already-dead animals. Maybe they did both.

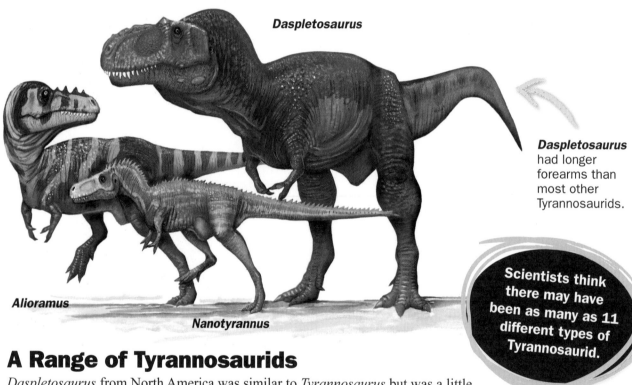

Daspletosaurus

Alioramus

Nanotyrannus

Daspletosaurus had longer forearms than most other Tyrannosaurids.

Scientists think there may have been as many as 11 different types of Tyrannosaurid.

A Range of Tyrannosaurids

Daspletosaurus from North America was similar to *Tyrannosaurus* but was a little smaller and had a heavy head with fewer but larger teeth. At about 6 metres (20 ft) long, *Alioramus* was a medium-sized tyrannosaurid from Asia. It had a long skull with knobbles and spikes along the top. The smallest was *Nanotyrannus*, from Montana, USA, which was about 4 metres (13 ft) long. Experts are undecided about this last one. Some think it may have been a small *Albertosaurus*, but the one skull available to study was certainly from an adult animal.

Triassic	Early/Mid Jurassic	Late Jurassic	Early Cretaceous	Late Cretaceous
245–208 MYA	208–157 MYA	157–146 MYA	146–97 MYA	97–65 MYA

Tyrant Lizard King

Tyrannosaurus, the biggest of the tyrannosaurids, is often known by its full species name *Tyrannosaurus rex* or simply *T. rex*. Other dinosaurs also have full species names, such as *Allosaurus atrox*, *Velociraptor mongoliensis* and so on, but these are usually only used by scientists.

Tyrannosaurus rex was a fearsome predator.

Frightful Bite

Tyrannosaurus had incredibly powerful jaws and teeth used to rip flesh from its prey. Gouges in the pelvic bone of a late Cretaceous specimen of the three-horned dinosaur *Triceratops* exactly match the size and spacing of the teeth of *Tyrannosaurus*. From these marks scientists could tell that a Tyrannosaurus bit down into the meat of the hind leg and tore it away from the bone when the *Triceratops* was already dead. But whether or not it was the *Tyrannosaurus* that killed it, nobody can tell.

Coprolite

Fossilized animal droppings are known to geologists as coprolites and they give useful clues to an extinct animal's diet. But, as with footprints, it is often impossible to tell what animal made which coprolite. Big coprolites, more than 20 centimetres (8 in) long, that may have come from *Tyrannosaurus*, have been found to contain smashed-up undigested bone fragments.

Footprint

In the late 1980s, a dinosaur footprint almost 1 metre (3 ft) long was discovered on a slab of late Cretaceous rock in New Mexico. Whatever beast made it had a meat-eater's claws. There was only one print, so the stride of the animal must have been greater than the almost 3-metre (10-ft) long slab of rock. Scientists estimate the animal was moving at 8–10 km/h (5–6 mph). We cannot be sure this footprint was made by *Tyrannosaurus*, but we know of no bigger meat-eating dinosaurs in Cretaceous America.

The New Kings

What was the biggest, strongest and fiercest meat-eating dinosaur that ever lived? *Tyrannosaurus*? Not any more! For the past hundred years we have said that *Tyrannosaurus* was the most powerful of the meat-eating dinosaurs. Generations of scientists have believed this to be so and have even stated that it would be mechanically impossible for bigger meat-eating animals to have existed. But now, the remains of even bigger meat-eaters are being found. In the 1990s, the skeletons of two carnivorous dinosaurs were found within a year of one another: one in South America, the other in Africa. Although neither skeleton was complete, they appear to have belonged to a group of dinosaurs that were even longer than *Tyrannosaurus*.

See page 200 for a chance encounter between *Kaprosuchus* and *Carcharodontosaurus*.

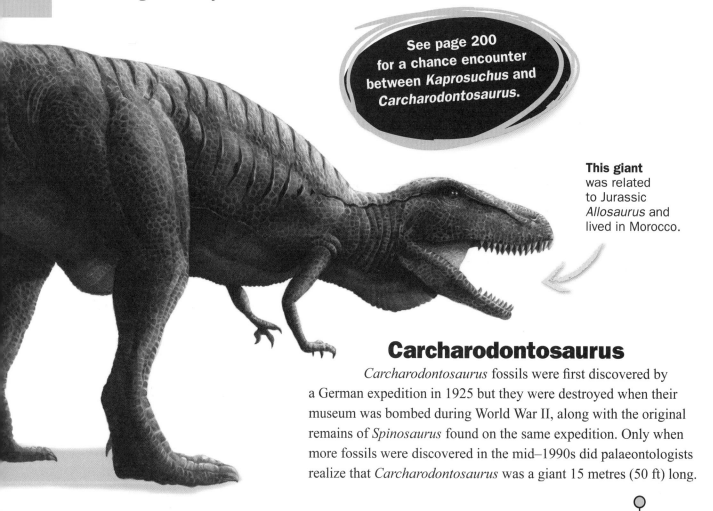

This giant was related to Jurassic *Allosaurus* and lived in Morocco.

Carcharodontosaurus

Carcharodontosaurus fossils were first discovered by a German expedition in 1925 but they were destroyed when their museum was bombed during World War II, along with the original remains of *Spinosaurus* found on the same expedition. Only when more fossils were discovered in the mid–1990s did palaeontologists realize that *Carcharodontosaurus* was a giant 15 metres (50 ft) long.

Triassic	Early/Mid Jurassic	Late Jurassic	Early Cretaceous	Late Cretaceous
245–208 MYA	208–157 MYA	157–146 MYA	146–97 MYA	97–65 MYA

Monstrous Skull

The skull of *Carcharodontosaurus* is almost completely known. When putting the skull bones together, the scientists only had to recreate the missing front of the snout and the bones at the very rear. This they could do by drawing on their knowledge of other skulls. The final skull is 1.5 metres (5 ft) long and had strong, curved, shark-like teeth. We know far less about the skull of *Giganotosaurus*. What we can be sure of, however, is that the jaws were not as powerful as those of *Tyrannosaurus*, the teeth were not as strong and it had an even smaller brain than the Tyrant Lizard King.

Giganotosaurus

Giganotosaurus seems to have been closely related to *Carcharodontosaurus*, even though it lived in isolated South America in the late Cretaceous period while the other lived in Africa. It is likely that, in the early part of the Cretaceous period, before the continents were separated by oceans, the ancestors of these animals spread across the whole world. After the continents split apart, *Giganotosaurus* began to evolve separately.

Comparing Kings

Both *Carcharodontosaurus* and *Giganotosaurus* were longer than the previous record-holder *Tyrannosaurus*. However, as shown above only *Tyrannosaurus* is known from complete skeletons and there is still a lot we don't know about the other two. Even so, *Tyrannosaurus* seems to have been a much heavier animal and was higher at the hip, so we could still say that the biggest meat-eating dinosaur that is completely known is *Tyrannosaurus*. Still the king!

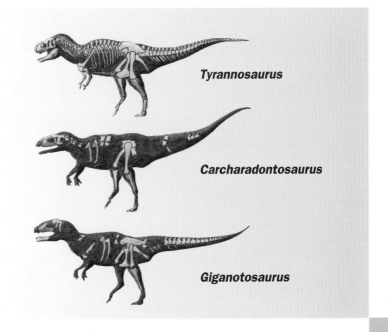

Tyrannosaurus

Carcharadontosaurus

Giganotosaurus

The Truth About Carnivores

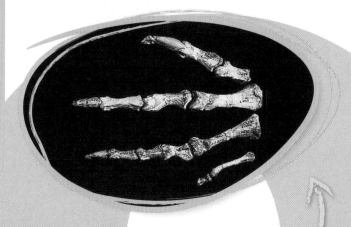

Q: Were dinosaur chicks looked after by their parents?

A: *Oviraptor* chicks were precocial – that means that they could take care of themselves as soon as they hatched. In a single clutch the individual eggs hatched at different times over several days, so the new chicks were not all hunting for the same food at the same time.

Q: How did *Velociraptor's* killer claw work?

A: *Velociraptor's* second toe had a huge claw that was used for killing. Its joints were like those of a cat's and could lift the huge claw out of the way when walking. *Velociraptor* attacked with the claws of all four limbs and could even jump up onto the back of its prey.

Q: Were all carnivores hunters?

A: Scientists believe that some carnivores, including *Dilophosaurus*, fed on carrion – that is, the carcasses of dead animals – rather than hunting down live prey. They think this because dinosaurs like *Dilophosaurus* had much shorter claws than other deadly predators of the time.

Q: Did *Tyrannosaurus rex* have a strong bite?

A: *T. rex* had massive jaws with very powerful muscles, which means that it could bite straight through even the biggest bones. Some of its teeth could reach 30 centimetres (12 in) in length.

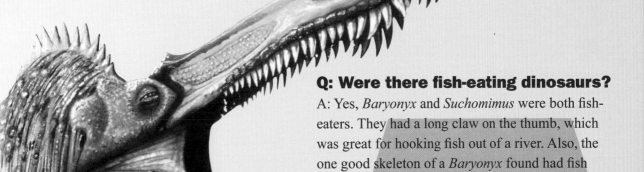

Q: Were there fish-eating dinosaurs?

A: Yes, *Baryonyx* and *Suchomimus* were both fish-eaters. They had a long claw on the thumb, which was great for hooking fish out of a river. Also, the one good skeleton of a *Baryonyx* found had fish scales in its stomach.

Q: Did dinosaurs hunt by smell?

A: We do not know this for sure, but probably not. It is really only mammals that hunt by smell.

Q: What colour were carnivores?

A: They may have been striped and spotted, like today's tigers and leopards. If so, this camouflage would have been useful when they were hunting.

Q: Is it true that dinosaurs had feathers

A: The meat-eating dinosaurs are closely related to modern birds and it is true that some of the smaller ones were covered in feathers. People found this hard to believe, until many fossils dinosaurs and birds were found in China in the 1990s. Some of these fossils were preserved in such detail that they even show the feathers.

The **stegosaurids** were all **heavily** armoured.

Chapter 2:
Herbivores

Enter into the fascinating world of the **plant-eaters**. These ancient creatures of the Reptile Age included enormous **sauropods, crest-headed duckbills** and **spiky nodosaurids.** Just how many plants did the largest herbivores need to eat each day, in order to fuel their **massive** bodies? Why did some of them have such heavy plates, spikes, clubs and fins? Who were their **worst enemies?** And what tactics did they employ to protect themselves and their young? Using the various **fossils** discovered around the world, **scientists** have been able to make informed guesses about this diverse group of dinosaurs. Read through this chapter to learn more about their incredible findings.

The First Plant-Eating Dinosaurs

Plant-eating dinosaurs (herbivores) were the real giants of the Age of the Dinosaurs. They numbered the mighty *Diplodocus* and *Seismosaurus* among their ranks, the largest animals ever to walk the Earth. Herbivorous reptiles are known from the early part of the Age of Reptiles 350 million years ago. The first herbivorous dinosaurs evolved in the late Triassic period, appearing about the same time as the carnivores. Because the hipbones in both groups of dinosaurs are similarly formed, we know that the plant-eaters must have evolved from meat-eating dinosaurs.

Plateosaurus

The first plant-eating dinosaurs belonged to the prosauropod group. *Plateosaurus* was a typical prosauropod. It had a long neck and small head, but perhaps its most important feature was its big body. To process plant matter a herbivore needs a far greater volume of digestive gut than a carnivore. The prosauropod's heavy mass of intestines, carried well forward of the hips, would have made the animal too unbalanced to spend much time on its hind legs, so prosauropods became four-footers early in their history.

Triassic	Early/Mid Jurassic	Late Jurassic	Early Cretaceous	Late Cretaceous
245–208 MYA	208–157 MYA	157–146 MYA	146–97 MYA	97–65 MYA

Developing Vegetation

In the early part of the Reptile Age the most prolific plants were a kind of a fern that had seeds. They were the primary food source of the main plant-eating animals, the mammal-like reptiles. The seed ferns died away during the Triassic period, and ferns more like our modern species became common. Another group of reptiles, the rhynchosaurs, evolved to eat them. At the end of the Triassic period, conifer trees spread everywhere and prosauropod dinosaurs evolved to eat them.

Mussaurus

The smallest dinosaur skeleton known belongs to a prosauropod. *Mussaurus* is small enough to be held in the the palm of a human hand. But we know it is the skeleton of a baby because the eyes and feet are bigger in relation to its body size than they would be in an adult, and its bones are not totally fused together. An adult *Mussaurus* would have been about 3 metres (10 ft) long.

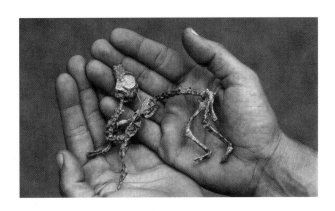

Skull Comparision
Between a Herbivore and Carnivore

Plateosaurus
- Jaw articulates below level of teeth.
- Leaf-shaped teeth with continuous cutting edge.
- Coarsly-serrated teeth for shredding leaves and shoots.
- Teeth more or less the same size.

Tyrannosaurus
- Jaw articulates at point level with teeth.
- Strong, spike-shaped piercing teeth used for gripping and killing.
- Finely-serrated saw-edged teeth like a steak knife.
- Teeth often break off and new ones grow in their place, creating a snaggle-toothed appearance.

Life of the Prosauropods

Ever since plants have existed plant-eating animals have fed on them, and ever since plant-eating animals have existed meat-eaters have, in turn, fed on them. This type of food chain can still be seen today on the grasslands of Africa where herds of herbivorous wildebeest and zebra graze on the low vegetation of the savannah and, in turn, are preyed upon by prowling carnivores such as lions and cheetahs. It was no different during the age of the dinosaurs. Prosauropods fed on the trees and were themselves stalked by the meat-eaters of the time, including the early carnivorous dinosaurs.

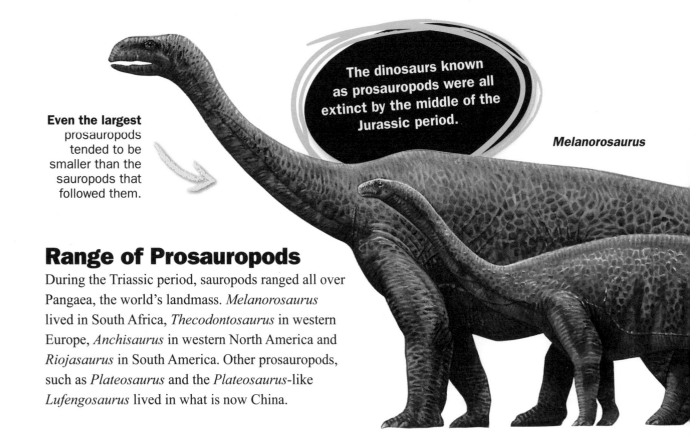

Even the largest prosauropods tended to be smaller than the sauropods that followed them.

The dinosaurs known as prosauropods were all extinct by the middle of the Jurassic period.

Melanorosaurus

Range of Prosauropods

During the Triassic period, sauropods ranged all over Pangaea, the world's landmass. *Melanorosaurus* lived in South Africa, *Thecodontosaurus* in western Europe, *Anchisaurus* in western North America and *Riojasaurus* in South America. Other prosauropods, such as *Plateosaurus* and the *Plateosaurus*-like *Lufengosaurus* lived in what is now China.

Triassic	Early/Mid Jurassic	Late Jurassic	Early Cretaceous	Late Cretaceous
245–208 MYA	208–157 MYA	157–146 MYA	146–97 MYA	97–65 MYA

Helpless Prey

Palaeontologists have found the remains of a prosauropod *Euskelosaurus* in late Triassic rocks in South Africa and Switzerland. The bones of its feet and legs are preserved, but the rest of the skeleton is broken up and scattered. Teeth of crocodile-like reptiles and carnivorous dinosaurs are among them. From this we suppose that *Euskelosaurus* became stuck in mud, and while struggling helplessly, was attacked by meat-eaters.

Trackways

An artist's impression of a footprint. The footprints called Navajopus from early Jurassic rocks of Arizona perfectly match the foot bones of a typical prosauropod, with the big hind feet and smaller front feet, each with four toes and inwardly-curved claws. They are likely to have been made by a small *Thecodontosaurus*-sized prosauropod called *Ammosaurus*.

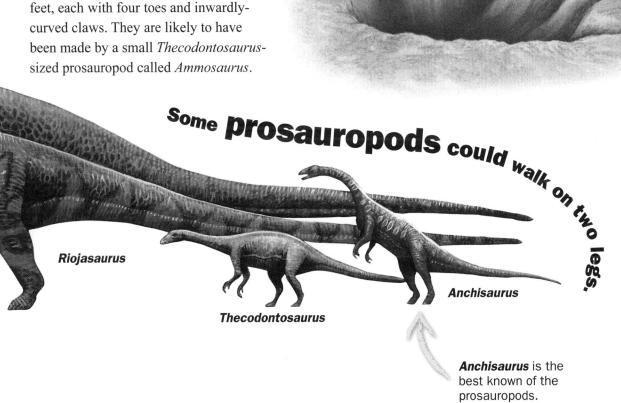

Some **prosauropods** could walk on two legs.

Riojasaurus

Thecodontosaurus

Anchisaurus

Anchisaurus is the best known of the prosauropods.

Sauropods

The biggest of all the dinosaurs were the long-necked plant-eaters known as sauropods (lizard feet). These creatures had elephantine bodies, legs like tree trunks, relatively small heads on top of long necks and long, whip-like tails. They were related to the meat-eating dinosaurs and to the prosauropods, evolving in the early Jurassic, peaking in the late Jurassic and dying off in Cretaceous times. We used to think that sauropods were too heavy to spend much time on land, and must have supported their vast bulk by wading in deep water. However, we now know (mostly from fossilized footprints) that sauropods moved about in herds on dry land.

Sauropods were able to stand up on their hind legs to reach tall branches to feed from.

Triassic	Early/Mid Jurassic	Late Jurassic	Early Cretaceous	Late Cretaceous
245–208 MYA	208–157 MYA	157–146 MYA	146–97 MYA	97–65 MYA

In Defence

Sauropods would have been prey to the big carnivorous dinosaurs. Just as today tigers do not attack fully-grown elephants, in Jurassic times the biggest of the sauropods would have been safe from the meat-eaters but the young and the sick would have been under threat. *Diplodocus* probably protected itself and its herd by using its long tapering tail as a whip. *Shunosaurus*, which lived in China during the middle Jurassic, probably used the small club on the end of its tail to defend itself.

Diplodocus

Perhaps the best known of the long sauropods is *Diplodocus*. At 27 metres (88 ft) long, it was one of several sauropods that roamed the plains and woodlands of North America in late Jurassic times. The way the neck bones were articulated tells us they browsed on low ferny vegetation, probably sweeping out great arcs with their long necks. The balance of muscles at the hips would also have enabled them to stretch up on their hind legs to reach the trees. The signs of wear on their teeth show they fed in both positions.

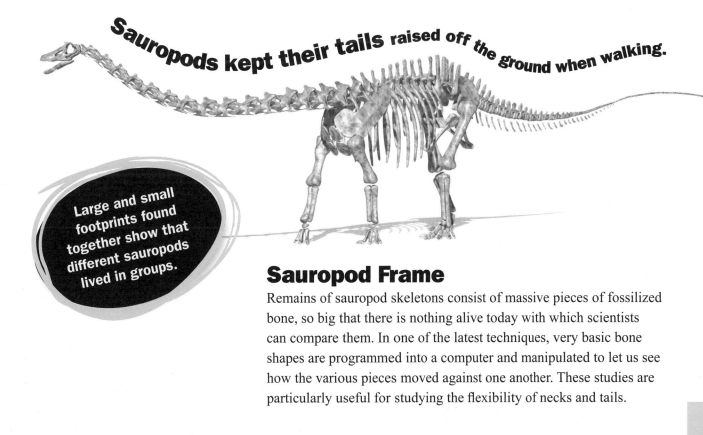

Sauropods kept their tails raised off the ground when walking.

Large and small footprints found together show that different sauropods lived in groups.

Sauropod Frame

Remains of sauropod skeletons consist of massive pieces of fossilized bone, so big that there is nothing alive today with which scientists can compare them. In one of the latest techniques, very basic bone shapes are programmed into a computer and manipulated to let us see how the various pieces moved against one another. These studies are particularly useful for studying the flexibility of necks and tails.

20th-century Dinosaur Discoveries

1900 *Brachiosaurus* found in Colorado by Elmer Riggs.

1901 Yale Peabody Museum mounts a skeleton of *Edmontosaurus* – the first dinosaur to be mounted in America.

1905 Carnegie Museum in Pittsburgh makes casts of its complete *Diplodocus* skeleton and distributes it to the major museums of the world.

2000 Nate Murphy finds a duckbilled *Brachylophosaurus* skeleton that shows skin, muscle and even stomach contents.

1995 Largest theropod *Giganotosaurus* found in Argentina.

1986 Joint Chinese-Canadian expeditions begin in Asia.

1909 The great dinosaur deposits of Canada begin to be uncovered.

1907–1910 Eberhard Fraas of Stuttgart Museum collects dinosaurs in Tanzania (then German East Africa), including that of *Brachiosaurus* – the biggest mounted skeleton known.

1923 Roy Chapman Andrews of the American Museum of Natural History finds the first dinosaur nests and eggs in Mongolia.

At the beginning of the 20th century, dinosaur science was an established field of study. The emphasis gradually changed from a 'big game hunt' in which wonderful specimens were obtained to show off, to more serious scientific study.

1951 Chinese expedition uncovers the big dinosaur deposits in central China.

1980 Luis and Walter Alvarez propose the theory of the asteroid impact to explain dinosaur extinction.

1975 Debate over warm-bloodedness, led by Robert Bakker begins.

1957 Structure of dinosaur bones gives the first indication that they may have been warm-blooded.

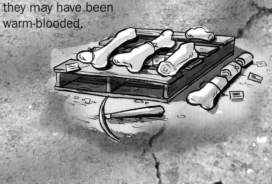

The Heyday of the Sauropods

During the late Jurassic period, sauropods were at their most prolific and widespread. Some were long and low, and browsed the low vegetation. Others were tall and browsed the lower branches of trees. There were two main types, distinguished by the shape of their teeth. *Diplodocus* and the other long, low sauropods had peg-like teeth; while the taller stouter sauropods, such as *Brachiosaurus*, had thick, spoon-shaped teeth that indicate a different type of feeding arrangement. However, nobody is yet sure what it was.

Seismosaurus

The longest dinosaur known is *Seismosaurus*. Imagine *Diplodocus*, then double its length. Make this length by stretching the neck and the tail in proportion to the body and this is what *Seismosaurus* looked like. So far, only one *Seismosaurus* skeleton has been found – in the Morrison Formation rocks in New Mexico.

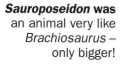

***Sauroposeidon* was** an animal very like *Brachiosaurus* – only bigger!

Dinosaur Detectives

Comparing isolated bones to those of more complete skeletons can give us some idea of the kind of animal they came from. In 1999, four neck vertebrae of a gigantic sauropod turned up. The *Sauroposeidon* bones turned out to be very similar to the neck bones of *Brachiosaurus*.

Triassic	Early/Mid Jurassic	Late Jurassic	Early Cretaceous	Late Cretaceous
245–208 MYA	208–157 MYA	157–146 MYA	146–97 MYA	97–65 MYA

Apatosaurus Growth Rate

It is difficult to tell how long a dinosaur lived. Sometimes, growth lines in the bones (like the rings of trees) suggest the animal grew more quickly at some time of each year. Its age can be assessed by counting the lines. Studies of the bones of *Apatosaurus*, the relative of *Diplodocus*, suggest that these sauropods grew quickly, without growth rings, for about 10 years. By then, they had reached 90 per cent of their adult size. After they reached this age, they grew very little.

Seismosaurus may have measured **50** metres (164 ft) long.

The ground must rocked with *Seismosaurus* on the move. Its name means Earth-shaking Lizard.

Visitors marvel at the sheer size of *Brachiosaurus* at the Natural History Museum in Berlin

Brachiosaurus

Although many remains have been found in the Morrison Formation, the best skeleton of *Brachiosaurus* was found halfway across the globe in Tanzania. This shows that in late Jurassic times Pangaea had not yet split up completely and the same types of dinosaur lived all over the world. A German expedition unearthed this skeleton in 1909, when Tanzania was still called German East Africa. The complete skeleton, the biggest mounted anywhere, is in the Natural History Museum in Berlin.

The Last of the Sauropods

As the world passed from the Jurassic into the Cretaceous period, the vegetation began to change and the continents to move apart. Different dinosaurs were becoming prominent. The sauropods began to die away as a completely different group of plant-eating dinosaurs evolved. In some places the sauropods still thrived, either because the old style vegetation still flourished in some environments, or because they lived on isolated continents where the new dinosaurs did not reach. Despite the spread of the new dinosaur types there were sauropods existing right to the very end of the Dinosaur Age.

Dressed to Impress

Amargasaurus from early Cretaceous Argentina had a double row of spines down its neck and a tall fin down its back. Unusual sauropods evolved in Cretaceous South America because it was an island continent at the time, and evolution took an independent direction there.

Not only did the late sauropods have armour, but some of them had spines and frills as well.

Triassic	Early/Mid Jurassic	Late Jurassic	Early Cretaceous	Late Cretaceous
245–208 MYA	208–157 MYA	157–146 MYA	146–97 MYA	97–65 MYA

Argentinosaurus

To date, the heaviest dinosaur ever found is *Argentinosaurus*. We have only six vertebrae, a part of its hips, a bit of rib and a leg bone. The leg bone is as tall as a man. From this we deduce the animal was about 27 metres (88 ft) long and weighed about 50,000 kilograms (110,000 lbs). Like some earlier Morrison Formation sauropods, *Argentinosaurus* had vertebrae made of thin struts and sheets of bone with great hollows between them – a strong but light construction, vital for such a huge animal.

The bony armour pieces from the back of a titanosaurid were found as long ago as 1890 in Madagascar.

Saltasaurus

Of the sauropods that survived into the Cretaceous period the titanosaurids (such as *Saltasaurus*) were perhaps the most successful. Despite their name, at about 12 metres (39 ft) long, they were not particularly big for sauropods. In recent years, it has been found that at least some titanosaurids had a back covered in armour. This may not have been for defence but, like the shell on the back of a crab, it might have been for stiffening the backbone to help the animal carry its weight. The palaeontologist who first identified the armour in 1890 was not believed, and it was only with the discovery of armoured titanosaurids in Argentina in the 1970s and a more complete armoured titanosaurid in Madagascar in the 1990s this his theory was proven to be correct.

Saltasaurus was native to Argentina in South America.

Jurassic World

By the time of the Jurassic period (208–146 million years ago), Pangaea had begun to break up. New oceans began to form and shallow seas spread over the continental lowlands. The opening of the continents formed a seaway all around the world in the regions of the Equator. Constant westward-flowing currents along this seaway led to milder and moister climates.

The Jurassic period was the great age of the **large herbivores,** including *Apatosaurus, Diplodocus* and *Brachiosaurus.*

In 1795 the word **'Jurakalk'** first appeared in scientific papers. It comes from the Jura Mountains in Switzerland, where limestone's from the period were studied.

Insects thrived during this period and the first bird, *Archaeopteryx* appeared.

There was probably more **oxygen** and **carbon dioxide**, encouraging both animal life and plant growth.

61

Ornithopods – the Bird Feet

Another group of plant-eating dinosaurs developed during the Triassic period, whose arrangement of bones in the hip gave more space for the big gut needed by plant-eaters, yet enabled them to balance on their hind legs. As a result, most of these animals were two-footed herbivores. Victorian scientists called the long-necked plant-eaters the sauropods (lizard feet) because they had a lizard-like arrangement of bones in their feet; the two-footed, bird-hipped dinosaurs they called the ornithopods (bird feet). We still use these terms today.

Hypsilophodon

From a distance a small ornithopod may have looked rather like a small carnivorous dinosaur. However, there were important differences: it had a much bigger body to hold the plant-digesting guts, and a head with a beak and cheek pouches. The arms were also different, having four or five fingers rather than two or three like meat-eaters. The markings were also probably quite different, far more subdued than those seen on carnivorous dinosaurs.

The ornithopods appeared at about the same time as the meat-eating dinosaurs and the prosauropods.

Hypsilophodon **was an** agile runner and grew to around 2 metres (6.6 ft) in length.

Triassic	Early/Mid Jurassic	Late Jurassic	Early Cretaceous	Late Cretaceous
245–208 MYA	208–157 MYA	157–146 MYA	146–97 MYA	97–65 MYA

Heterodontosaurus Skull

The skull of an ornithopod was significantly different from that of a sauropod. There was always a beak at the front for cropping the food. The teeth were not merely for raking in leaves but were designed for chewing them, either by chopping or grinding. Depressions at each side of the skull show where there were probably cheek pouches, used to hold the food while it was being processed. This is a far more complicated arrangement than that of the prosauropods and sauropods.

Three Kinds of Teeth

In 1976, the complete skeleton of a primitive early ornithopod *Heterodontosaurus* was discovered in South Africa. Strangely, it had three different types of teeth: sharp cutting teeth at the front, a pair of dog-like fangs in both upper and lower jaw, and broad grinding teeth. No other ornithopod had such teeth. It is almost as if evolution were trying out new designs early in the development of the group before natural selection determined the best pattern. Later, more advanced ornithopods had quite complex chewing mechanisms. An animal like *Iguanodon* or a hadrosaur had its upper teeth mounted on articulated plates at each side of the skull. As the lower jaw rose these plates moved outwards to allow the sloping chewing surfaces of both sets of teeth to grind past one another. This constant milling action wore away the teeth, and new ones grew to replace them.

Hipbones

As with the prosauropods the hipbones of the sauropods incorporated a pubic bone that pointed down and forward. This meant the big plant-digesting intestines had to be carried forward of the hips. In ornithopods this pubic bone is swept back, except for a pair of forward extensions that splayed out to the side. The big plant-digesting intestines could be carried beneath the animal's hipbone, closer to its centre of gravity. This enabled the ornithopod to walk on its hind legs, balanced by its tail – just like a meat-eating dinosaur.

The Iguanodon Dynasty

Iguanodon was among the first dinosaurs to be discovered. Its remains came to light about the same time as those of the meat-eater *Megalosaurus*. The teeth and a few scraps of bone were found first and were obviously from a very large plant-eating reptile. At the time, few people were familiar with modern plant-eating reptiles, so the animal was particularly unusual. Some scientific work was being done on the modern South American plant-eating lizard, the iguana, which had teeth rather like those of this new fossil – hence, its name, *Iguanodon*.

Meet the Family

The modern interpretation of *Iguanodon* is that, as an adult, it was too heavy to spend much time on its hind legs, so went about mostly on all fours. Since it was discovered, scientists have found many more closely-related iguanodontids. Australian *Muttaburrasaurus* was slightly smaller and had a high ridge on its nose. American *Tenontosaurus* had a particularly long tail. The most primitive member of the group was *Gasparinisaura* from Argentina, which was only the size of a turkey.

> All known members of the Iguandon family lived during the Cretaceous period.

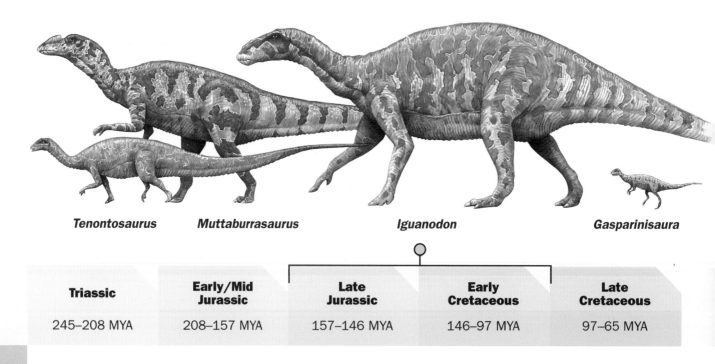

Tenontosaurus   Muttaburrasaurus   Iguanodon   Gasparinisaura

Triassic	Early/Mid Jurassic	Late Jurassic	Early Cretaceous	Late Cretaceous
245–208 MYA	208–157 MYA	157–146 MYA	146–97 MYA	97–65 MYA

Iguana Tooth

The first remains of *Iguanodon* – teeth and parts of bones – were discovered in Kent in about 1822 by English country doctor Gideon Mantell and his wife Mary. Other scientists of the day thought they were the teeth of fish, or of a hippopotamus. But Mantell realized the teeth were from a plant-eating reptile like a modern iguana lizard. His first reconstructions showed a kind of a dragon-sized, iguana-like reptile, similar to the first reconstructions of the meat-eating *Megalosaurus*, also recently discovered.

The Ouranosaurus Question

One iguanodontid, *Ouranosaurus*, had an arrangement of tall spines forming a kind of a wicket fence along its backbone, probably to support some sort of fin or sail. As *Ouranosaurus* lived in North Africa, which was hot and arid during Cretaceous times, such a sail could have regulated its body temperature by exposing blood vessels to the warming sun and cooling wind. A meat-eater, *Spinosaurus*, lived in the same time and place and also had a sail. Another theory is that the spines supported a fatty hump, such as camels have today.

No one is quite certain of the function of the sail or fin on *Ouranosaurus's* back.

Iguanodon probably grazed on horsetails.

Changing Face

Over the years, as more specimens were found, *Iguanodon's* appearance changed. In the 1850s, it was constructed in the Crystal Palace gardens, south London, along the lines of Mantell's big lizard. Then, in 1878, a whole herd of *Iguanodon* skeletons, mostly complete, were found in a coal mine in Bernissart, Belgium. These animals were up to 10 metres (33 ft) long and had hind legs that were much longer than their forelimbs. This evidence led to reconstructions of *Iguanodon* sitting on its hind legs, resting on its tail like a kangaroo – an image that was accepted for the next century.

The Duckbills

In the later Cretaceous period, a new group of ornithopods evolved from the iguanodontids. The vegetation was changing: primitive forests were giving way to modern-looking woodlands of oak, beech and other broad-leaved trees with clusters of conifers and undergrowths of flowering herbs. These new dinosaurs, the hadrosaurs, spread and flourished in the broad-leaved forests throughout Europe, Asia and North America. They had thousands of grinding teeth and the front of the mouth supported a broad beak. These dinosaurs took over from the sauropods in terms of importance.

Hadrosaurus

Hadrosaurus was, like *Iguanodon*, essentially a two-footed plant-eating dinosaur, which, as an adult, would have been rather too heavy to spend much time on its hind legs. So it would have moved about on all fours for much of the time. *Hadrosaurus's* tail was very deep and flat which once led scientists to think the hadrosaur may have been a swimming animal – an idea that has now been discarded. The *Hadrosaurus's* most distinctive feature, was its broad, flat, duck-like beak.

See what happens when *Gorgosaurus* stumbles into a herd of *Parasaurolophuses*, on page 186

Unlike many other duckbills, *Hadrosaurus* did not have a crest.

Hadrosaurus had fleshy, weight-bearing pads on its forelimbs, presumably for walking on all fours.

Triassic	Early/Mid Jurassic	Late Jurassic	Early Cretaceous	Late Cretaceous
245–208 MYA	208–157 MYA	157–146 MYA	146–97 MYA	97–65 MYA

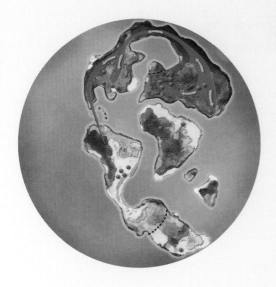

Spread of Duckbills

The hadrosaurs spread from Europe and became the most important plant-eating dinosaurs in the northern hemisphere. At the time, Europe, Asia and North America were joined in a single landmass and animals could spread freely. However, South America was an island continent separated from North America by a wide seaway. Hadrosaurs did reach South America but never gained a secure foothold. Long-necked sauropods remained the most important plant-eaters in South America until the end of the Dinosaur Age.

At up to 1.8 metres (6 ft) long, the crest of a *Parasaurolophus* was the biggest of all hadrosaur crests.

Head Crests

Some hadrosaurs, such as this *Parasaurolophus*, were quite striking because of their elaborate head crests. Mostly made of hollow bone connected to the nostrils, they were probably used for making noises to signal to one another through dense forests. Each type of hadrosaur had a unique crest shape, so that different herds could be distinguished from one another. Those with flat heads or solid crests probably supported an inflatable flap of skin that could have been puffed up like a frog's throat to make a noise.

Modern Conifers

Modern conifers, such as pine and spruce, as well as the broad-leaved trees, such as oak and ash, appeared in Cretaceous times. Until then, the more primitive conifers, such as monkey puzzle trees, had sustained the sauropods. Hadrosaurs were well-equipped for dealing with the new conifer trees. They used their broad beaks to scrape off the needles and their batteries of teeth to grind them down before swallowing.

67

The Plated Lizards

Not long after the ornithopods came into existence, all kinds of other dinosaurs began to evolve from them. Many of these dinosaurs sported armour of one kind or another, and they were too heavy to spend much time on two legs. They became mostly four-footed beasts. One of the groups had armour arranged in a double row of plates or spikes down its back and tail. These plated dinosaurs were known as stegosaurs. One of them, *Stegosaurus*, lived in North America at the end of the Jurassic period. We know it was a big four-footed animal, up to 8 metres (26 ft) long, with shorter legs at the front.

Bony Plates

A double row of plates stuck up along the back of a *Stegosaurus*, and two pairs of spikes stuck out on either side towards the tip of its tail. The head of a *Stegosaurus* was particularly small and held a very small brain. As with ornithopods and their relatives it had a beak at the front of the mouth and probably cheeks along the side.

Some scientists think the plates were covered in horn and formed an armoured shield. Others insist the plates were covered in skin and acted as heat exchangers. On cool days, they absorbed warmth, while on hot days, the animal could have cooled its blood by turning the plates into the wind.

Triassic	Early/Mid Jurassic	Late Jurassic	Early Cretaceous	Late Cretaceous
245–208 MYA	208–157 MYA	157–146 MYA	146–97 MYA	97–65 MYA

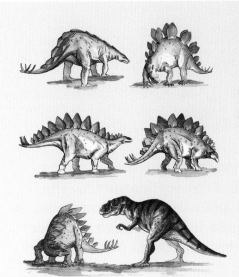

Plate Puzzles

The back plates of *Stegosaurus* were embedded in its skin but not attached directly to its skeleton. This has caused uncertainty about how they were arranged. One theory suggests the plates lay flat as armour along the animal's back. Another is that they stood upright in pairs. Yet another says they had a single upright row of overlapping plates. The most widely accepted view is that they stood in a double row, alternating with one another.

Turn to page 150 to see what happens when *Stegosaurus* comes under attack from *Allosaurus*.

Death of Denver Stegosaurus

A team from the Denver Museum, USA, discovered a *Stegosaurus* skeleton by accident while excavating another dinosaur. This *Stegosaurus* had a diseased tail after a broken tail spike became infected. The weakened animal then died during a drought. Its internal organs rotted and its stomach bloated, rolling it over on to its back. The drought ended and a nearby river burst its banks, covering the *Stegosaurus* with silt. All this was deduced 140 million years later from the fossil and the types of rocks found nearby. Such study of the lead-up to fossilization is known as taphonomy.

The *Stegosaurus* is weakened by the infection in its tail and stumbles to the ground.

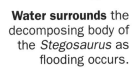

Water surrounds the decomposing body of the *Stegosaurus* as flooding occurs.

As the *Stegosaurus* continues to decompose, its bones become buried in silt.

A World of Stegosaurids

Stegosaurus **was not the only stegosaurid. There were many others, and they probably evolved from an early Jurassic group called the scelidosaurids. The most primitive of the stegosaurids we know were found in middle Jurassic rocks in China. From such medium-sized animals developed the wide range of plated and spiked dinosaurs that were important in late Jurassic times. By the middle Cretaceous they had all but died out. The remains of an animal that may have been a stegosaurid was found in late Cretaceous rocks in India. Perhaps the group lasted longer in India which was an island continent at the time.**

Variety of Stegosaurids

The most primitive stegosaurid known is the 4-metre (13-ft) long *Huayangosaurus* from middle Jurassic China. Its armour included paired narrow back spikes and a tail with two pairs of spikes. It also had a pair of shoulder spikes, as did some later stegosaurids. *Dacenturus* from late Jurassic Europe had low rounded plates on its shoulders and back, and tall spikes all down its tail. Late Jurassic *Kentrosaurus* from Africa had its centre of gravity at its hips, so, like some sauropods, it could rise on its hind legs to browse. *Wuerhosaurus* from early Cretaceous China was as big as *Stegosaurus* and had long low back plates.

Huayangosaurus had four legs of equal length.

Kentrosaurus   Dacenturus

Triassic	Early/Mid Jurassic	Late Jurassic	Early Cretaceous	Late Cretaceous
245–208 MYA	208–157 MYA	157–146 MYA	146–97 MYA	97–65 MYA

An Early Stegosaurid

Cow-sized *Scelidosaurus*, known from the early Jurassic rocks of England, was a four-footed herbivore covered in small studs of armour. It may have been an ancestor of the stegosaurids; or of the later Cretaceous nodosaurids of America, and the middle Jurassic to late Cretaceous ankylosaurids of Europe, North America and Asia. It may even have been ancestral to both.

Stegosaurus Skeleton

Stegosaurus had strong hips and hind legs, showing that it could rear up on two legs to eat leaves from tree branches.

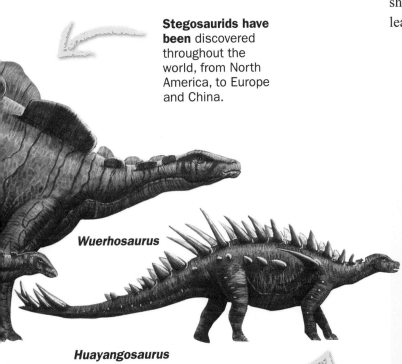

Stegosaurids have been discovered throughout the world, from North America, to Europe and China.

Wuerhosaurus

Huayangosaurus

Stegosaurids tended to have shorter front legs than back legs.

Clever Tail

Most stegosaurids had two pairs of spikes at the end of their tail. The tails were usually quite flexible and could have been swung sideways with some force against the flanks of an attacker. There was a gap in the hipbones that may have held a concentration of nerves to control the hind legs and tail, and a gland that supplied extra energy. This space in the tail gave rise to a once-popular misconception that stegosaurids had two brains.

The Nodosaurids – Spiky Dinosaurs

As the Jurassic period passed, the armoured stegosaurids became extinct and other groups of armoured dinosaurs evolved. The two most closely related groups were the nodosaurids and the ankylosaurids. Each had small bony plates across their broad backs. These plates stretched up the neck to the head and down the tail, and would have had horny covers that made the animal's back impregnable. The distinctive feature of the nodosaurid group was the presence of long robust spikes sticking out sideways and upwards from the shoulders and from the sides.

Spiky Customers

Two related groups of armoured dinosaur existed in Cretaceous times. The nodosaurids were characterized by spikes on the neck and sides; the ankylosaurids had clubs on the ends of their tails.

Heavy armour: An ankylosaurid (top) and a nodosaurid (bottom).

Sauropelta

One of the earliest nodosaurids was *Sauropelta* from Montana and Wyoming, USA. It had an arched back, long tail, and hind legs that were longer than its fore legs. Like all other nodosaurids its neck, back and tail were covered in armour. *Sauropelta's* long defensive spines were confined to the neck and shoulders, and spread outwards and upwards. At 5 metres (16 ft) long, *Sauropelta* was an average size for a nodosaurid.

Triassic	Early/Mid Jurassic	Late Jurassic	Early Cretaceous	Late Cretaceous
245–208 MYA	208–157 MYA	157–146 MYA	146–97 MYA	97–65 MYA

Sauropelta Skeleton

The solid back plate armour is the most commonly fossilized part of a nodosaurid, and is usually found upside-down. If a nodosaurid died and fell into a river, it may have been washed out to sea. As it decayed, expanding digestive gases in its gut would have turned it over, its heavy back acting as a keel. It would be buried in the seabed and eventually fossilized in that position.

Struthiosaurus

Not all nodosaurids were big animals. *Struthiosaurus* from late Cretaceous rocks of central Europe was only 2 metres (6.5 ft) long, with a body the size of a dog. It appears to have been an island-dweller. Animals tend to evolve into smaller forms on islands to make the best use of the limited food stocks. A modern example would be the tiny Shetland pony from the islands off Scotland.

See how *Gastonia* fares when attacked by sickle-clawed *Utahraptor*, page 182.

Gastonia's spikes could be 30 cm (12 in) tall.

Gastonia

One of the best-preserved nodosaurid fossils ever found was that of *Gastonia*. Its armour was tightly-packed, forming a solid shield over the hips. Spikes stood up over the shoulders, and it had a series of broad flat spines, almost blades, sticking outwards and running down each side from the neck to the tip of the tail. It was found in early Cretaceous rocks in Utah, USA, but an almost identical dinosaur from the same period has been found in England.

The Ankylosaurids – the Club-tails

The ankylosaurids were closely related to the nodosaurids but mostly came later, towards the end of the Cretaceous period. With their armoured necks and backs, they looked very like their relatives but instead of having spikes on the shoulders and the sides they had a different weapon – a heavy bony club at the end of the tail. This could have been devastating when swung at an enemy. It is also possible that the club may have been used as a decoy. Perhaps the club on the tail looked like a head on a neck, and caused meat-eaters to attack it instead of the more vulnerable front end.

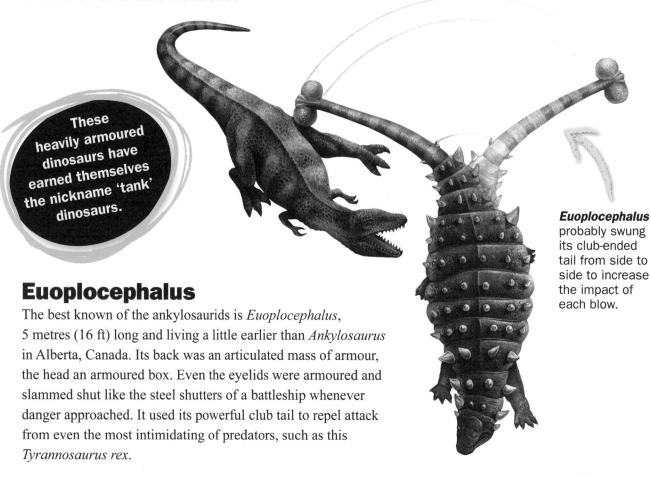

These heavily armoured dinosaurs have earned themselves the nickname 'tank' dinosaurs.

Euoplocephalus probably swung its club-ended tail from side to side to increase the impact of each blow.

Euoplocephalus

The best known of the ankylosaurids is *Euoplocephalus*, 5 metres (16 ft) long and living a little earlier than *Ankylosaurus* in Alberta, Canada. Its back was an articulated mass of armour, the head an armoured box. Even the eyelids were armoured and slammed shut like the steel shutters of a battleship whenever danger approached. It used its powerful club tail to repel attack from even the most intimidating of predators, such as this *Tyrannosaurus rex*.

Triassic	Early/Mid Jurassic	Late Jurassic	Early Cretaceous	Late Cretaceous
245–208 MYA	208–157 MYA	157–146 MYA	146–97 MYA	97–65 MYA

Cretaceous Undergrowth

By the end of the Cretaceous period, modern plants had evolved. Beneath the broad-leaved trees was an undergrowth of flowering herbs such as buttercups. The ankylosaurids and the nodosaurids carried their heads low and their mouths close to the ground. They were evidently low-level feeders that ate these flowering herbs.

Euoplocephalus had **huge** *defensive spikes.*

A powerful tail club could weigh as much as 20 kilograms (44 lbs).

Tail Club

The tail of *Euoplocephalus* and other ankylosaurids had a heavy club at the end. To support it the vertebrae of half the tail were fused together in a solid bar, making it like the shaft of a medieval mace. The muscles at the broad hips and the flexible part of the base of the tail would have allowed this club to be swung sideways with great force against the legs and flanks of a raiding meat-eating dinosaur, breaking bones and crippling the attacker for life.

A Hearty Appetite

Without its armour we can see that *Euoplocephalus* was a heavy four-footed animal. Its hips were broad but the design allowed the guts to be carried well back. The guts would have been massive and probably contained fermenting chambers like those of modern cows.

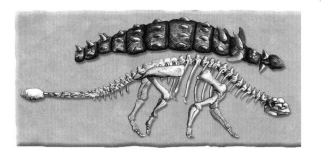

Boneheads

Imagine a dinosaur, a two-footed plant-eating dinosaur such as an ornithopod, but give it a very high forehead. What you would have is a pachycephalosaurid – another dinosaur group descended from the ornithopods. We think the mass of bone on top of the head was used as a weapon – a kind of battering ram. This was probably not for use against predators but for display purposes in courtship battles. There was a great range of sizes in pachycephalosaurids. The largest known, at 5 metres (16 ft) long, was North American *Pachycephalosaurus*. The smallest was *Micropachycephalosaurus* from China, which was about the size of a rabbit. This smallest of dinosaurs has the longest dinosaur name ever given.

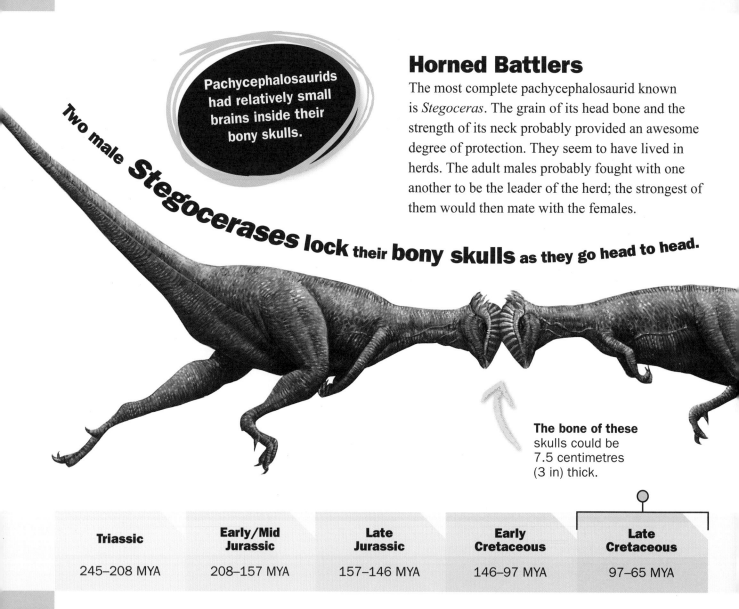

Pachycephalosaurids had relatively small brains inside their bony skulls.

Two male Stegocerases lock their **bony skulls** as they go **head to head.**

Horned Battlers

The most complete pachycephalosaurid known is *Stegoceras*. The grain of its head bone and the strength of its neck probably provided an awesome degree of protection. They seem to have lived in herds. The adult males probably fought with one another to be the leader of the herd; the strongest of them would then mate with the females.

The bone of these skulls could be 7.5 centimetres (3 in) thick.

Triassic	Early/Mid Jurassic	Late Jurassic	Early Cretaceous	Late Cretaceous
245–208 MYA	208–157 MYA	157–146 MYA	146–97 MYA	97–65 MYA

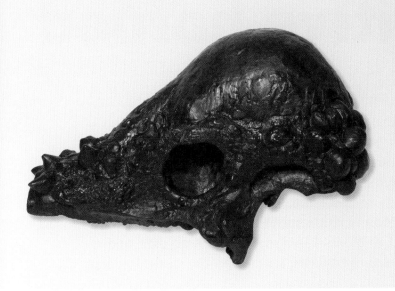

Hard Heads

Dinosaur skulls are rarely preserved as fossils, but pachycephalosaurid skulls were different. The top bone of the skull was so massive it often survived as a fossil. Commonly, the only part of the animal to be preserved, these skulls are often found very battered. This suggests they were washed down a river for long distances before being buried in sediment. This may mean they were mountain-living animals, like their modern counterparts – mountain sheep.

Modern Sparrers

In the American Rocky Mountains, modern bighorn sheep and mountain goats go through an annual ritual in which the males fight the flock leader to test his strength. The construction of their skulls and horns protects them from suffering much damage when they bash against one another. Pachycephalosaurids probably had similar rituals.

Meet the Boneheads

Each group of pachycephalosaurids had its own type of skull shape and ornamentation. *Stegoceras* and *Homalocephale*, from Mongolia, had sloping heads, higher at the rear, the latter with an elaborate head crest. *Prenocephale*, also from Mongolia, had a more rounded dome-like head. Both had decorative lumps around the bony crown. North-American *Stygimoloch* was perhaps the strangest, with a weird array of spikes and spines all around its dome. These were probably used for intimidation rather than fighting. All pachycephalosaurids lived in the late Cretaceous era.

77

The Primitive-horned Dinosaurs

The last of the plant-eating dinosaur groups existed from the mid- to late Cretaceous period. Like the ankylosaurids and nodosaurids they lived in North America and in Asia, and they also evolved from ornithopods. They were equipped with armour but it was confined solely to the head. Early types were lightly-built and very ornithopod-like, but in later forms the armour on the head became so heavy they went about as four-footed animals. Flamboyant neck shields and horns evolved and these horned dinosaurs became known as the ceratopsians.

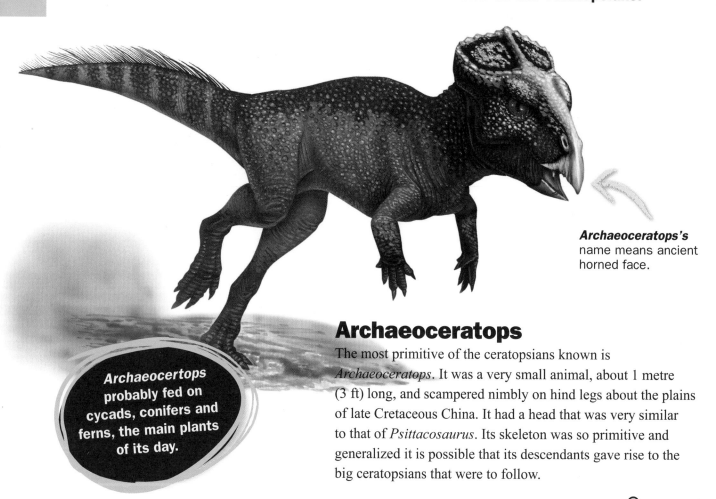

Archaeoceratops's name means ancient horned face.

Archaeocertops probably fed on cycads, conifers and ferns, the main plants of its day.

Archaeoceratops

The most primitive of the ceratopsians known is *Archaeoceratops*. It was a very small animal, about 1 metre (3 ft) long, and scampered nimbly on hind legs about the plains of late Cretaceous China. It had a head that was very similar to that of *Psittacosaurus*. Its skeleton was so primitive and generalized it is possible that its descendants gave rise to the big ceratopsians that were to follow.

Triassic	Early/Mid Jurassic	Late Jurassic	Early Cretaceous	Late Cretaceous
245–208 MYA	208–157 MYA	157–146 MYA	146–97 MYA	97–65 MYA

A **fossil** of a cycad leaf.

Ceratopsians would have used their narrow beaks to clip tough cycad leaves.

Cycad Fossil

At the end of the Cretaceaous period the old-style vegetation was largely replaced by modern species of plants. However, some of the older types of palm-like cycads remained in some regions. In the areas where they occurred the ceratopsians may have relied on these plants. Their narrow beaks would have reached into the palm-like clump of fronds and selected the best pieces, and their strong jaws would have shredded them.

Big Brother

By the time *Montanoceratops* had evolved, towards the end of the late Cretaceous, the ceratopsians were bigger and had developed the horns on their head. *Montanoceratops* was about 3 metres (10 ft) long and walked on all fours. However, like its two-footed ancestors, it still had claws on its feet. In later ceratopsians the toenails developed into hooves, better able to take the weight of big animals.

An Early Sheep

Scientists regard *Protoceratops* as the sheep of late Cretaceous Mongolia. Similar in size, they lived in herds and grazed the sparse vegetation of the arid landscape. One particular skeleton had the skeleton of a fierce carnivore, *Velociraptor*, clinging to its head shield. The meat-eater had attacked the ceratopsian with its killing claws, but the ceratopsian must have fought back with its big beak as both dinosaurs lost their lives during the fight.

Who's a Pretty Boy?

An early relative of the ceratopsians was the 1.5 metre (5 ft) long parrot-lizard *Psittacosaurus*. It developed a very strong beak and powerful jaws for plucking and chopping tough vegetation. A bony ridge around the back of the skull anchored its strong jaw muscles. The bony ridge and its big beak gave its skull a square shape, and the head must have looked very like the head of a modern parrot.

79

The Big-horned Dinosaurs

The big ceratopsians were probably the most spectacular dinosaurs of the late Cretaceous period. They were all four-footed animals, mostly as big as today's rhinoceros. The ridge of bone around the neck had evolved into a broad shield. They also had an array of long horns on the face. The skulls of the big ceratopsians were so solid and tough that they were often preserved as fossils. As a result, we know a lot about their heads. There were two main lines of evolution. One group developed long frills and a pair of long horns above the eyes; the other had shorter frills and tended to have a single horn on the nose.

Triceratops

The biggest and most famous of the ceratopsians is *Triceratops*. Although it belonged to the short-frilled lineage that tended to have horns only on the nose, *Triceratops* also had long horns above its eyes. It grew to about 9 metres (29 ft) long and weighed up to 6,000 kilograms (13,225 lbs). Several species of *Triceratops* roamed the plains between Alberta, Canada, and Colorado, USA, at the end of the Cretaceous period. Like all ceratopsians, it had a shield, probably used to protect its neck and shoulders, but it may also have been used for display or heat regulation.

Triceratops means 'three-horned face'. The name refers to the three long horns on its nose and brows.

Triceratops had small horns on its cheeks

Triassic	Early/Mid Jurassic	Late Jurassic	Early Cretaceous	Late Cretaceous
245–208 MYA	208–157 MYA	157–146 MYA	146–97 MYA	97–65 MYA

Migrating Herds

We know ceratopsians moved about in herds because we have found bone beds consisting of many hundreds, even thousands, of skeletons. The animals would have been migrating to areas where there was more food at a particular time of year. When crossing a river they may have been caught by a sudden flash flood that washed them away. This still happens in Africa today as herds of wildebeest migrate from one feeding ground to another.

All For One

The horns of ceratopsians would have been used to defend themselves and their herd against big carnivores and also to tussle with one another over position in the herd. Having locked horns, they would have pushed and shoved until one of them gave way. Little harm would have come to the loser. While travelling, the ceratopsians may have kept their young at the centre of the herd to protect them. If attacked by carnivores they may have formed a circle with the youngsters in the centre and the adults facing outwards so that the attackers were faced with the shields and horns of all the herd. Today, musk-oxen protect their herd in this way.

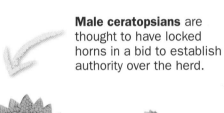

Male ceratopsians are thought to have locked horns in a bid to establish authority over the herd.

Variety of Heads

Ceratopsians all had the same body shape, but their different shapes of shield and horn arrangements made each type easily recognizable to their own herd. *Chasmosaurus* (pictured top) had an enormous, sail-like shield. *Styracosaurus* (pictured bottom) had a monumental horn on its nose and an array of horns around its shield. *Einiosaurus* had a long nose horn that curved forwards, while *Achelousaurus* had a battering ram on its nose, a pair of short, blade-like horns above its eyes, and a curved pair at the shield-edge.

The Truth About Herbivores

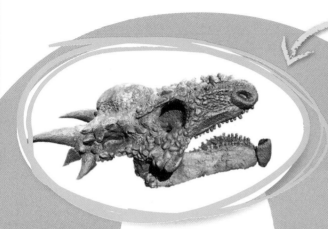

Q: How did *Iguanodon* chew its food?

A: The bones of the upper jaw were only loosely fixed to the skull. As the lower jaw came up, it pushed these jawbones outwards, so that the banks of teeth ground past each other. Cheek pads held the food in place while this was happening.

Q: Did all herbivores have long necks?

A: Not all of them no. This fossil shows that *Brachytrachelopan*, and several other dinosaurs, had a short neck. Rather than reaching up to high branches to feed, *Brachytrachelopan* must have eaten plants growing on the ground, right in front of it.

Q: What did *Stegosaurus* use its plates for?

A: Although the real purpose of the plates running down *Stegosaurus's* back is not known, some scientists believe they were used as some sort of temperature control. When the weather was cold, *Stegosaurus* would have stood sideways to the sun, so sunlight could warm its plates. In the heat, *Stegosaurus* is believed to have cooled off by facing its plates into the wind.

Q: Why are there so few marks left by tails?

A: We used to think that sauropods lived in water and that the tails floated. Now it seems that these huge animals kept their tails clear of the ground using tendons and muscles.

Q: Why are the skulls of the boneheads more frequently found than others?

A: Apart from those of horned dinosaurs and boneheads, dinosaur skulls were made from delicate struts of bone, loosely joined together. Soon after death, the skulls simply fell to pieces and scattered. Bonehead skulls were so solid, however, that they are frequently found as fossils, even thought the rest of the skeleton has disappeared.

Q: What did *Triceratops* use its huge frill for?

A: The frill probably evolved among the early ceratopsians as a ridge to hold the neck muscles. Then it became a shield to protect the neck, and was probably brightly coloured to act as a signal flag to other dinosaurs.

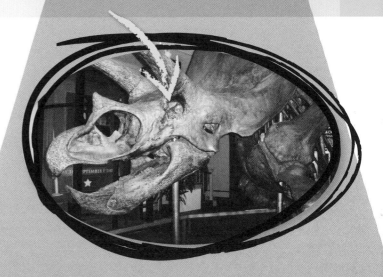

Q: Do fossils show what kind of food a dinosaur ate?

A: A coprolite is a fossil of an animal's meal, still in its stomach. The skeleton of the ankylosaur, *Minmi*, from Australia contained a coprolite – a rare find for a herbivore. The animal had been eating ferns and primitive flowers just before it died.

Q: How did sauropods breathe?

A: Scientists think that the giant sauropods breathed like birds, rather than using the fleshy lungs of mammals. Birds keep the air circulating throughout the body, and hold it in air sacs and hollow bones. An efficient system like this would be needed for something as big as *Apatosaurus*.

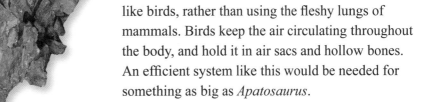

Proganochelys was the world's earliest turtle.

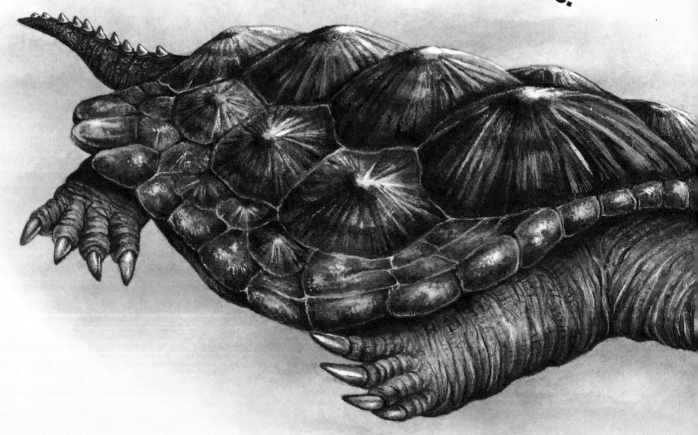

Chapter 3:
In the Sea

What was happening in
the **world's oceans** when the
mighty dinosaurs were roaming the planet?
Discover all there is to know about the **ancient
marine creatures** of the Reptile Age, and see
how they range from the world's **first turtle** to the
massive, short-necked pliosaurs and the curious-looking, long-
necked elasmosaurs. Which reptiles became stealthy predators?
How did the **fastest** swimmers move through the water?
Why did some sea creatures swallow stones? Thanks to a
wealth of **fossil evidence**, scientists have been
able to build an incredible picture of underwater life
all those millions of years ago. Look through this
chapter to read all about what they
have discovered.

The First Swimmers

All life came from the sea. It has been estimated that life appeared about 3,500 million years ago, and only relatively recently did it come out on to land (about 400 million years ago for plants and 300 million years ago for animals). Some of the first land creatures were to evolve into reptiles and the dinosaurs. But the ways of evolution are devious. Almost as soon as land life had become established, there was a tendency for a return to the sea to exploit new food sources. As early as 250 million years ago, there were water-living animals that had evidently evolved from land-living ancestors even before the dinosaurs.

A Freshwater Puzzle

Mesosaurus was a freshwater reptile, about one metre (3 ft) long, with a flattened swimming tail and powerful webbed hind legs. It probably used its tail and hind legs to drive itself through the water, and steered and stabilized itself with its webbed front feet. The odd thing about it, though, is the fact that its skeletons are found in early Permian rocks in both South Africa and Brazil. Scientists wondered how the remains of a freshwater animal were fossilized on two widely separated continents. It was the first piece of evidence in support of a revolutionary concept called 'plate tectonics'. In Permian times, when *Mesosaurus* was alive, there was no Atlantic Ocean. What is now Africa and South America were part of a single vast landmass call Pangaea. The same kinds of animal lived all over the world because there were no oceans to separate them.

Mesosaurus had fine, needle-like teeth – probably for filtering invertebrates from the water to eat.

Carboniferous	Permian	Triassic	Early/Mid Jurassic	Late Jurassic
360–286 MYA	286–248 MYA	245–208 MYA	208–157 MYA	157–146 MYA

Retro Pioneer

Spinoaequalis was the earliest-known land animal to re-adapt itself to a water-living existence. It was a lizard-like beast found in late Carboniferous marine sediments of Kansas in the United States. Its name means 'equal spine', which refers to the strong spines on the tail that made a flat vertical paddle and allowed for the attachment of strong muscles – in short, the tail of a swimming animal. Aside from this feature, *Spinoaequalis* had the skeleton of a land-living creature.

The Buoyancy Problem

Hovasaurus from late Permian rocks found in Madagascar had a swimming tail twice the length of the rest of its body. It was so long that it would have been difficult to use on land. However the feet were those of a land-living reptile. Most skeletons of *Hovasaurus* have pebbles lying in the stomach area. Evidently this animal swallowed stones to adjust its buoyancy underwater. This is one of the swimming techniques used by animals whose ancestors were land-living animals.

Hovasaurus was just 50 centimetres (20 in) long.

A Modern Example

The Galapagos marine iguana looks and lives very much like some of these early swimming reptiles. It has adopted a partially aquatic way of life because it feeds on seaweed. Its lizard body, legs and feet show that it is a land-living animal, but its long, muscular, flexible tail is ideal for swimming. It also has the ability to hold its breath for long periods under water and a method for removing from its system excess salt absorbed from the seawater. These are adaptations that can never show up on fossil animals, so we do not know if early swimming reptiles had them or not.

A Shoal of Swimming Reptiles

From fossils, we know that many sea creatures were in fact reptiles that had left dry land for a new life in the water. If there was more food in the water than on land, and if there were fewer dangerous predators in the sea, an aquatic life would have become enticing. Reptiles can adapt quite easily to such a lifestyle. They have a low metabolic rate and they can cope without oxygen for some time. In addition, moving around in the water takes only about a quarter of the energy of moving about on land.

An Early Winner

A broad body shape is adequate for a slow-moving animal, but such a creature remains vulnerable to attack. This threat encouraged the development of armour in such reptiles. The end result was the turtle. The earliest turtle, *Proganochelys*, dates from the late Triassic period, and lived in Germany. Its body shape and the arrangement of the shell is very similar to the modern turtle, which has not evolved much in 215 million years.

Big is Beautiful

The biggest turtle known, *Archelon*, cruised the inland sea that covered much of North America in late Cretaceous times. At almost 4 metres (13 ft) long it was bigger than a rowing boat. Its shell was reduced to a system of bony struts covered by tough skin; much like the biggest of the modern turtles, the leatherback. It probably fed on soft things like jellyfish, as just like the modern leatherback, its jaws were not very strong.

Carboniferous	Permian	Triassic	Early/Mid Jurassic	Late Jurassic
360–286 MYA	286–248 MYA	245–208 MYA	208–157 MYA	157–146 MYA

A Modern Turtle

The turtle is a slow-moving aquatic reptile, shelled above and below, with paddle limbs that allow it move through the water with a flying action. Protected from its enemies and surrounded by sources of food, it needs neither speed nor a streamlined body shape to thrive.

Life after death

The science of taphonomy deals with what happens to an animal after it dies, and how it becomes a fossil. At sea this can be relatively simple.

In an environment in which sediment is constantly accumulating, creatures have a better chance of being fossilized.

1. When an animal dies it may float at the surface for a while until the gases generated in its decaying tissue disperse.

2. Eventually, however, it sinks to the bottom of the sea. A less buoyant animal may go straight to the bottom. There, it may be scavengend by bottom-living creatures, and its parts broken up and dispersed.

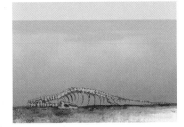

3. If sand and mud are being deposited rapidly on the sea bed at the time, the body is quickly buried before too much damage is done.

4. After millions of years the sand and mud will be compressed and cemented together as rock, and the bones of the dead animal will have been replaced by minerals. It will have become a fossil.

Placodonts – the Shell-Seekers

There are all kinds of reasons why water-living animals should evolve from land-living animals. Most persuasive of these is the idea that when a good food supply exists, then nature will develop something to exploit it. Shellfish represent one such food supply. The earliest group of reptiles that seemed to be particularly well adapted to feeding on shellfish were the placodonts. Although they still needed to come to the surface to breathe, they rooted about on the bed of the Tethys Sea that spread across southern Europe in Triassic times.

A Shelled Family

Because they were slow moving animals, the placodonts must have been very vulnerable to the meat-eaters of the time. Many developed shells on their backs as protection. In some types, the shells were very extensive and looked very much like those of turtles, but the two groups of animals were in no way related. The similar shells developed independently among animals that had the same lifestyle in the same environment – a process known as 'convergent evolution'.

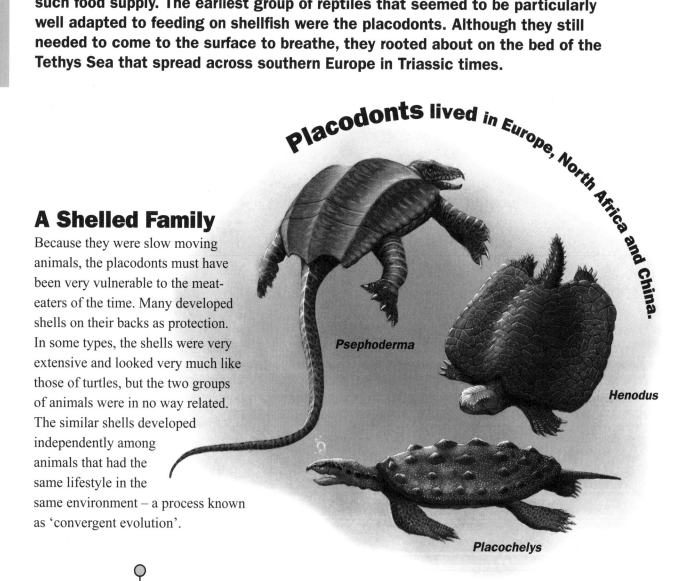

Placodonts lived in Europe, North Africa and China.

Psephoderma

Henodus

Placochelys

Triassic	Early/Mid Jurassic	Late Jurassic	Early Cretaceous	Late Cretaceous
245–208 MYA	208–157 MYA	157–146 MYA	146–97 MYA	97–65 MYA

Powerful Bite

From below, the protruding front teeth of *Placodus* are obvious. These were used for plucking the shells from the rocks and the seafloor. Further back the jaws have strong crushing teeth, and even the palate has a pavement of broad flat teeth, all ideal for smashing up the shells of shellfish. Holes in the side of the skull show where very powerful jaw muscles were attached. *Placodus* would have eaten bivalves similar to those that survive today, and brachiopods.

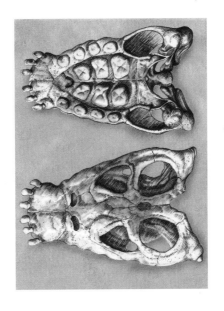

Placodus skull: The illustrations show the skull from below (top) and above.

Placodus had a chunky body, a paddle-shaped tail, webbed feet and a short head.

Placodus

The most typical of the placodonts was *Placodus* itself. In appearance it looked rather like an enormous newt, about 2 metres (7 ft) long.

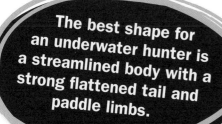

The best shape for an underwater hunter is a streamlined body with a strong flattened tail and paddle limbs.

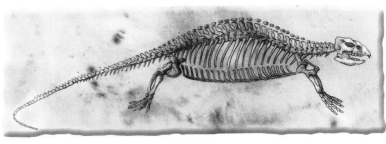

Built For Buoyancy

A glimpse of the skeleton of *Placodus* reveals one of its main adaptations to its underwater way of life – 'pachystosis'. This means that the bones were broad and heavy, perfect for feeding on the bottom of the ocean. Animals that have pachystosis also have big lungs to help to regulate their buoyancy. To accommodate its huge lungs, *Placodus* developed a broad rib cage. A modern animal with these adaptations is the sea otter. Its weight and large lung capacity enable it to walk along the sea bed with ease, hunting shellfish. *Placodus* would have had the same lifestyle.

Between the Land & the Sea

The nothosaurs preceded the plesiosaurs, rulers of the late Jurassic and Cretaceous seas. Like the placodonts, they are known mostly from the sediments laid down in the Tethys Sea, an ancient ocean that lay in the position where the Mediterranean Sea occupies today. Their necks, bodies and tails were long and they had webbed feet (but could still walk on land). Their hind limbs were more massive than their front limbs and were used mostly for swimming.

A Variety of Nothosaurs

Nothosaurus (from which the group gets its name) was 3 metres (10 ft) long, and had a very long head with jaws full of little teeth. *Lariosaurus*, at 60 centimetres (24 in) one of the smallest nothosaurs, was very primitive and looked much like a land-living animal that happened to be swimming in the sea. Big *Ceresiosaurus*, on the other hand, had feet that were almost like paddles, and a small head on a long neck.

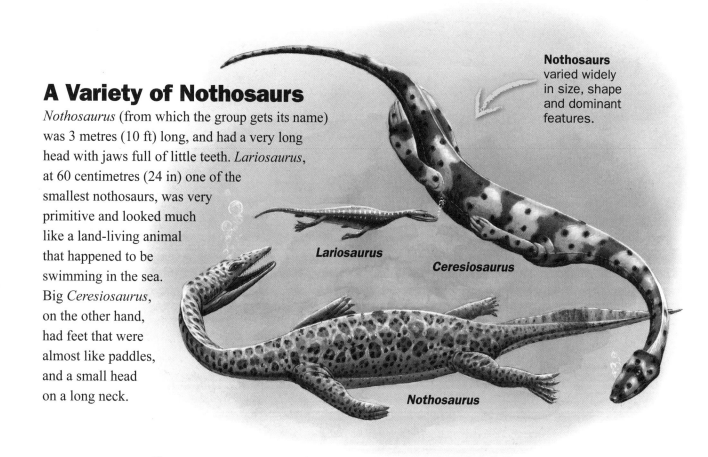

Nothosaurs varied widely in size, shape and dominant features.

Lariosaurus

Ceresiosaurus

Nothosaurus

Triassic	Early/Mid Jurassic	Late Jurassic	Early Cretaceous	Late Cretaceous
245–208 MYA	208–157 MYA	157–146 MYA	146–97 MYA	97–65 MYA

Duckbilled Platypus

The duckbilled platypus is an ancient animal with webbed feet that push the water back behind, driving the animal forward. Such a motion is quite primitive. Later marine animals had limbs that had evolved into flippers that were built like wings, allowing the animal to travel through the water in a flying motion. Nothosaurs share similarities with primitive platypus, but also with more advanced sea creatures. Some nothosaurs had webbed feet, while others had paddles.

Nothosaurs seem to represent a part-way stage between land-living animals and fish-eating seagoing ones like the plesiosaurs.

Nothosaurs
had many small pointed teeth in long narrow jaws for catching fish.

Nothosaur Fossil

Nothosaur fossils are known from the Alps and from China. Although these animals had legs and toes, their limb bones were not strongly joined to one another and the hips and shoulders were quite weak. This degenerate state shows that they were not well adapted for moving about on land and were better at swimming than walking.

Let's Go Fishing

The long jaws and sharp teeth of *Nothosaurus* were ideal for catching fish. The long neck would have been able to reach fast-swimming fish quickly, and the little teeth would have held the slippery prey firmly. These teeth can be seen in modern fish-eating animals like crocodiles.

The Giants of the Sea

The plesiosaurs were perhaps the most varied group of swimming reptiles during the time of the dinosaurs. They were ocean-going fish-eaters, ranging in size from the length of a small seal to that of a medium-sized whale. They had broad bodies, short tails and two pairs of wing-like paddles with which they flew through the ocean waters. One group had short necks and long heads, while the other had long necks and very small heads. The short-necked types are called the pliosaurs, and the long-necked types the elasmosaurs.

Underwater Attack

From the evidence available we can picture a late-Jurassic marine incident. A long-necked elasmosaur is feeding near the surface. A pliosaur cruises at some depth below, hunting fish and squid. Through the taste of the water it detects the presence of the other reptile. Vomiting out a few stomach stones it adjusts its buoyancy to allow it to rise. Then, when its prey is in view, it 'flies' towards it with strong thrusts of its flippers. Having secured a firm hold, the pliosaur twists its massive body, ripping the unfortunate elasmosaur apart before eating it.

Triassic	Early/Mid Jurassic	Late Jurassic	Early Cretaceous	Late Cretaceous
245–208 MYA	208–157 MYA	157–146 MYA	146–97 MYA	97–65 MYA

Big Mouth

The most spectacular feature of the skeleton of a pliosaur is its huge skull. The long jaws had many sharp teeth, ideal for catching big fish and squid and also for seizing larger prey. The nostrils are surprisingly small and would not have been used for breathing. Instead they would have been used for tasting the water and for judging the speed at which the animal was swimming. A pliosaur probably breathed through its mouth when it came to the surface.

Pliosaur Toothmarks

The limb bones of an elasmosaur found in late Jurassic marine rocks in Dorset, England, have given scientists a dramatic clue as to the feeding habits of the pliosaurs. Tooth marks punched deep into the bones match exactly the set of teeth of a big pliosaur. Until this discovery scientists thought that pliosaurs ate only fish and squid.

The pliosaurs were the largest of the plesiosaurs. They were the sperm whales of the Mesozoic seas.

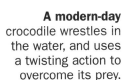

A modern-day crocodile wrestles in the water, and uses a twisting action to overcome its prey.

In For the Kill

At the back of the skull of a pliosaur are broad flanges. Scientists think these must have held massive neck muscles. This in turn suggests that pliosaurs were able to grab their larger prey, hold onto it and pull it to pieces using a strong thrusting or twisting action. Modern-day crocodiles hunting in deep water dismember their food in exactly the same way today.

A Range of Pliosaurs

We used to think that the pliosaurs were the biggest sea reptiles of all time. Nowadays we are finding the remains of beasts that were even bigger, yet the biggest of the pliosaurs were very big animals indeed. There were also many smaller pliosaurs. Their different sizes and head shapes reflected the different lifestyles and the different foods that they were eating. Some must have lived like penguins, darting and snatching at the weaving and dispersing fish shoals, but the biggest must have been the dolphins and toothed whales of their time. Often all that we know of a particular pliosaur is the skull. As all the bodies were built to a particular well-known plan, scientists assume that we know what the rest of the body was like. Sometimes that gives rise to misconceptions.

Monster of the Deep

We used to think that the skull of the pliosaur *Kronosaurus* represented less than one-quarter of the length of the whole animal, giving a total length of 12-14 metres (40–46 ft) – greater than the contemporary *Tyrannosaurus* on land. More recent studies suggest that the skull was about one-third of the total length, making it 8 metres (26 ft) long. Still quite a monster!

Kronosaurus probably fed on octopus and giant squid.

Triassic	Early/Mid Jurassic	Late Jurassic	Early Cretaceous	Late Cretaceous
245–208 MYA	208–157 MYA	157–146 MYA	146–97 MYA	97–65 MYA

Dolichorhynchops grew to be around 3 metres (10ft) long in total.

Super-penguins

Dolichorhynchops was a relatively small pliosaur that lived in the seas that covered late Cretaceous Manitoba in Canada. Judging by its build and its teeth, it swam agilely among the shoals of fish that frequented the waters, snapping them up in its long narrow jaws. It had the same kind of swimming technique as modern penguins, using paddles to get around.

Liopleurodon Tooth

This is the tooth of a *Liopleurodon*. It is about 20 centimetres (8 in) long. Bite marks found on the bones of the ichthyosaurs and other pleisiosaurs, show that *Liopleurodon* was a fierce predator.

A Half-way Stage

Fossilized bones of sea animals are often found on beaches, where the sea is eroding cliffs of Mesozoic rock, or in quarries. One of the most complete plesiosaur skeletons ever found was 5-metre (16-ft) long *Rhomaleosaurus*, uncovered in 1851 from stone quarries in Barrow upon Soar, Leicestershire, England. It was locally known as the 'Barrow Kipper' because of the appearance of its spread ribs, and has become the mascot of the village. Scientifically, the odd thing about *Rhomaleosaurus* is the fact that it has a long neck as well as a fairly large head. It is classed as a pliosaur, but it seems to be part-way between the short-necked pliosaurs and the long-necked elasmosaurs.

Fossilized bones of sea animals are much more common than those of land animals.

97

Cretaceous World

Landmasses were distinct continents during the Cretaceous period (146–65) million years ago. The movement of tectonic plates caused huge volcanoes to occur across the planet. Dinosaurs evolved into different species on each of the separate continents. The remains of 245 different dinosaur types have been discovered from the last 45 million years of the period – about half of all those known.

In the second half of the Cretaceous period, **flowering plants evolved.** There were forests of broadleaved trees, like those of today.

'Creta' is the Latin name for chalk. The chalk deposits of such places as the White Cliffs of Dover were formed at that time. The period was named in 1822.

The oceans were filled with all sorts of ancient, **predatory reptiles** like *Kronosaurus.*

The climate was **mild to tropical** over the whole of the world, with no permanent ice at the poles.

Elasmosaurs – the Long-necks

One early researcher described the long-necked plesiosaurs as 'snakes threaded through turtles'. Indeed, the broad body and the wing-like flippers are very reminiscent of the ocean-going turtle, but the long neck and the little head full of vicious pointed teeth are very different from those of the placid grazing shelled reptile that we know today. Elasmosaurs were the sea serpents of the time. They existed alongside the pliosaurs in the Jurassic and Cretaceous oceans.

Cryptoclidus

Cryptoclidus was a common elasmosaur found in late Jurassic rocks of Europe. Its mounted skeleton can be seen in several museums. It is typical of the whole elasmosaur group, with its broad body with ribs above and below, the long neck, the mouthful of sharp outward-pointing teeth and the paddles made up of packed bone.

Triassic	Early/Mid Jurassic	Late Jurassic	Early Cretaceous	Late Cretaceous
245–208 MYA	208–157 MYA	157–146 MYA	146–97 MYA	97–65 MYA

Underwater Flight

The plesiosaur paddle worked like a wing. Among the pliosaurs, the strongest muscles pushed the paddles forwards, so this must have been the power stroke. Among the elasmosaurs, there was as much muscle to pull the paddle back as there was to push it forward, allowing the body to turn very quickly. This suggests that the elasmosaurs had much more manoeuvrability than pliosaurs. Nowadays penguins use the same kind of swimming action.

Strong Swimmer

Cryptoclidus flew through the water. Its front paddles worked like wings, while the hind paddles acted as stabilizers.

The first named elasmosaur was *Elasmosaurus platyurus*. It was found in Kansas, USA.

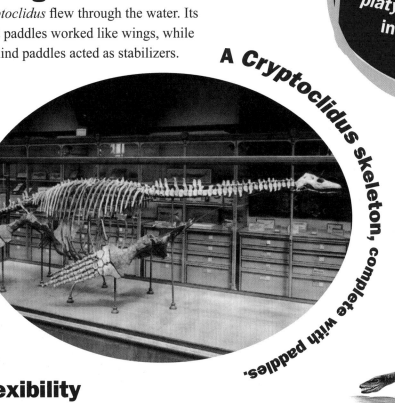

A *Cryptoclidus* skeleton, complete with paddles.

Most elasmosaurs had between 50 and 70 neck vertebrae.

Flexibility

The great length of the elasmosaur neck with its huge number of vertebrae have led some to suggest that it would be have been as flexible as a snake. But looking at the way the vertebrae are articulated, we can see that this was not quite true. From side to side there was quite a good degree of movement, but the neck was restricted in the up-and-down plane. Although an elasmosaur could reach downwards with ease, it could not hold its head up like a swan on the surface.

101

Elasmosaur Lifestyle

The elasmosaurs came in all sizes. As time went on there was a tendency for the group to develop longer and longer necks. It is likely that they hunted by ambush. The big body was probably used to disturb shoals of fish, while the little head at the end of the long neck then darted quickly into the group and speared individual fish on the long teeth. Moving the paddles in different directions would have turned the body very quickly into any direction. Their agility meant that they probably hunted on the surface as opposed to the pliosaurs, who were built for sustained cruising at great depths.

Elasmosaurus

We take the name of the elasmosaur group from the late Cretaceous *Elasmosaurus*. This had the longest neck, in proportion to the body, of any animal known. It had 71 vertebrae, in contrast to the 28 or so sported by the earlier elasmosaurs. This neck took up more than half of the length of the entire animal.

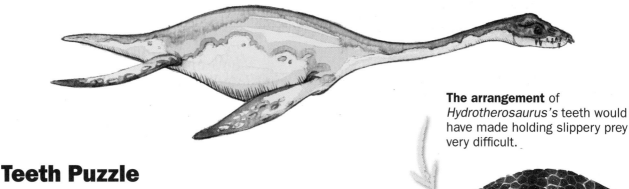

The arrangement of *Hydrotherosaurus's* teeth would have made holding slippery prey very difficult.

Teeth Puzzle

Most elasmosaurs had pointed teeth for catching fish. However, in *Hydrotherosaurus*, the teeth seem to be the wrong shape and jut outwards. It is possible that they used this tooth arrangement as a kind of a cage trap, to catch very small fish or invertebrates. On the other hand they could have used them as a rake for sifting through mud and sand on the sea bed.

Triassic	Early/Mid Jurassic	Late Jurassic	Early Cretaceous	Late Cretaceous
245–208 MYA	208–157 MYA	157–146 MYA	146–97 MYA	97–65 MYA

Surviving Today?

Now and again we hear stories of people sighting sea serpents that have a distinct similarity to plesiosaurs. Several photographs exist of rotting carcasses with a very plesiosaur look to them, but that usually turn out to be those of basking sharks. Although a basking shark looks nothing like a plesiosaur in life, its dead body deteriorates in a particular pattern. The dorsal fin and the tail fin fall off, losing the shark's distinctive profile. Then the massive jaws drop away. This leaves a tiny brain case at the end of a long string of vertebrae. Instant plesiosaur!

Elasmosaurs came ashore to lay eggs.

Giving Birth

Scientists cannot be sure that elasmosaurs laid eggs rather than giving birth to live young, but it is possible. Reptile eggs have hard shells through which the developing embryo can breathe. Unfortunately this means they cannot be laid at sea as the youngsters would drown. It is possible that elasmosaurs laid eggs the way modern turtles do, coming ashore at certain times of the year to scoop out a hole in the beach with their flippers.

The 'Polyphyletic' Theory

It is possible that the elasmosaurs were 'polyphyletic' – that means that they did not evolve from the one ancestor. The Jurassic elasmosaurs evolved from the same ancestors as the nothosaurs of the Triassic period. However, the arrangement of the skull bones of the Cretaceous elasmosaurs has led some scientists to suggest that these later ones actually evolved from the short-necked pliosaurs of the Jurassic period. The long neck developed independently in response to environmental pressures. Most scientists, however, believe that all the elasmosaurs evolved from the same ancestors – that is, they were 'monophyletic'.

Ichthyosaurs – the Fish Lizards

The most well-adapted marine reptiles of the Mesozoic were the ichthyosaurs. If you saw one swimming about you might easily mistake it for a dolphin or even a shark. It is all there – the streamlined body, the triangular fin on the back, the big swimming fin on the tail and the paired swimming organs at the side. Ichthyosaurs evolved in Triassic times and shared the Jurassic oceans with the plesiosaurs. They did not survive far into the Cretaceous period, however, and their places were taken by another group of marine reptiles – the mosasaurs.

A Clear Image

Thinly-layered late Jurassic rocks at Holzmaden in Germany are so fine that they contain the impressions of the softest organisms that lived and died there. The bottom of the sea (where the rocks formed) was so stagnant that nothing lived. Among the spectacular fossils found there are the ichthyosaurs, with indications of their soft anatomy still preserved. Flesh and skin still exist as a fine film of the original carbon. For the first time it was obvious that ichthyosaurs had a dorsal fin and a big fish-like fin on the tail.

Ichthyosaurs were descended from land-living animals and needed to come to the surface to breathe.

Triassic	Early/Mid Jurassic	Late Jurassic	Early Cretaceous	Late Cretaceous
245–208 MYA	208–157 MYA	157–146 MYA	146–97 MYA	97–65 MYA

Mary Anning

The Ichthyosaur Pioneer

As with the plesiosaurs, the ichthyosaurs were known before the dinosaurs. Early naturalists, who discovered them in eroding cliffs along the Dorset coast in southern England, took them for the remains of ancient crocodiles. Indeed their long jaws and sharp teeth are very reminiscent of crocodiles. Mary Anning (1799–1847), a professional fossil collector and dealer from Lyme Regis in Dorset, is credited with finding the first complete fossil ichthyosaur when she was 12 years old. Her work was crucial in furthering our knowledge of these creatures.

Ichthyosaur Skeleton

Entire skeletons of ichthyosaurs are relatively common, as these creatures were frequently fossilized. Many museums have complete ichthyosaur skeletons on display. This ichthyosaur is in the Bristol City Museum in England.

This fossil shows that **Ichthyosaurs** had **big** eyes.

A Modern Rendering

Now it is possible to paint an accurate picture of what an ichthyosaur looked like in life. From all the fossils we have found we know that they had streamlined, dolphin-like bodies, with fins on the back and tail. Unlike dolphins the tail fin was not horizontal but vertical. There were two pairs of paddles, the front pair usually bigger than the hind pair.

Mosasaurs

In 1770, workmen in a chalk quarry near Maastricht in Holland uncovered a long-jawed, toothy skull. Immediately the owner of the land sued for possession – a circumstance that is all too common in the field of palaeontology even today. Then, in 1794, the French army invaded. Despite the owner's attempt to hide the skull in a cave, it was seized as booty (with the help of a bribe of 600 bottles of wine) and taken back to Paris where it was studied by legendary French anatomist Baron Cuvier. By this time it had been identified as the skull of a huge reptile related to the modern monitor lizards. British geologist William Conybeare gave it the name *Mosasaurus* ('lizard from the Meuse').

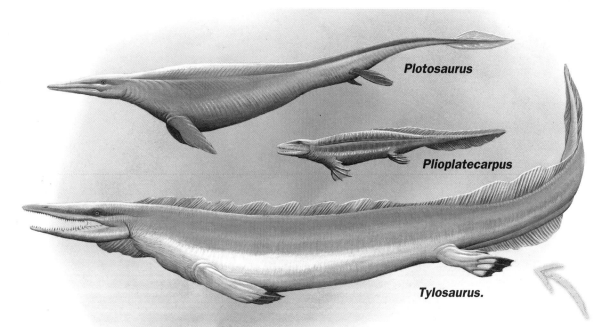

Plotosaurus

Plioplatecarpus

Tylosaurus.

A Range of Mosasaurs

Mosasaurs are known from late Cretaceous deposits throughout the world. They were all based on a similar body plan and ranged in size from a few metres to monsters 10 metres (33 ft) or more in length. Their heads were all very similar to those of the modern monitor lizard and their teeth had adapted to snatch at fish or ammonites. An exception was *Globidens*, which had flattened rounded teeth, which were obviously adapted for a shellfish diet.

Tylosaurus **was** one of the biggest Mosasaurs.

Triassic	Early/Mid Jurassic	Late Jurassic	Early Cretaceous	Late Cretaceous
245–208 MYA	208–157 MYA	157–146 MYA	146–97 MYA	97–65 MYA

Georges Cuvier

The jawbones of a completely unknown giant reptile unearthed from the underground quarries near the River Meuse convinced the French anatomist Baron Georges Cuvier (1769–1832) that there were once animals living on the Earth that were completely unlike modern types, and that these ancient animals were periodically wiped out by extinction events.

Mosasaurs had strong enough teeth to crunch through the shells of ammonites.

Dinner Time

There is direct evidence that mosasaurs ate the abundant ammonites of the time. The ammonites were relatives of the modern squid and nautilus, and sported coiled shells that are very common as fossils. They lived throughout the Mesozoic in the seas all over the world. One ammonite fossil has been found punctured by toothmarks that exactly match those of a small mosasaur. Evidently the reptile had to bite the ammonite sixteen times before crushing the shell and reaching the animal.

A modern-day **monitor** *lizard.*

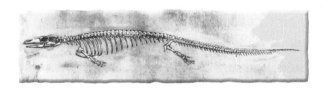

A Swimming Lizard

The aigalosaurs were ancesters of the mosasaurs. They were a group of swimming lizards from the late Jurassic and early to middle Cretaceous periods that lived in Europe. They grew up to one metre (3 ft) long, and had flattened tails but lacked the specialized paddle limbs of their descendants.

Family Member?

The bones of *Mosasaurus* were very similar to those of the modern monitor lizard. Despite extinction of individual species, the same lines of animals were continuing to develop into other forms. The concept of evolution that would explain such phenomena had not been developed when *Mosasaurus* was first studied by the early scientists.

Crocodiles

Crocodiles have remained essentially unaltered since late Triassic times. However, throughout their history there have been all kinds of specialist types. Some were long-legged and scampered about on land, while others ran about on hind legs like little versions of their relatives, the dinosaurs. More significantly, some developed into sea-living forms showing the same adaptations as other sea-living reptiles – the sinuous bodies, the paddle legs and the finned tails. These were particularly important in Jurassic times.

A Selection of Sea Crocs

Teleosaurus was a gharial-like sea crocodile, longer and slimmer in build than *Steneosaurus* (see opposite). *Metriorhynchus* was three metres (10 ft) long and shows much more extreme adaptations to a seagoing way of life. It lacked the armoured scales that we see on more conventional crocodiles. Its legs were converted into paddles that would have been almost useless on land. At the end of its tail the vertebral column was turned downwards, showing that it had a swimming fin like an ichthyosaur. *Geosaurus* was similar to *Metriorhynchus* but was later and slimmer, with narrow jaws.

Deinosuchus's name means Terrible Crocodile.

Teleosaurus

Metriorhynchus

Geosaurus

Triassic	Early/Mid Jurassic	Late Jurassic	Early Cretaceous	Late Cretaceous
245–208 MYA	208–157 MYA	157–146 MYA	146–97 MYA	97–65 MYA

Champosaur

Phytosaur

Crocodile

A Good Shape

Many semi-aquatic meat-eating reptiles have crocodile shapes. The champosaurs from the late Cretaceous period of North America were very crocodile-like and had the same lifestyle in the same habitat. The phytosaurs from the late Triassic period could be mistaken for crocodiles except for their nostrils, which were close to the eyes instead of at the tip of the snout. But these animals were not closely related to another. This is an example of parallel evolution.

Modern-day crocodiles are one-third the size of Deinosuchus.

The position of Steneosaurus's eyes (on the top of its head) suggests that it attacked shoals of fish from below.

Like Today's?

Looking at *Deinosuchus* from a distance you would think it was a modern crocodile. Indeed it belonged to the same family as modern crocodiles, although it lived in the late Cretaceous period. But then you notice its size – 15 metres (49 ft) long! This monster ate dinosaurs!

Steneosaurus

The fine shales that preserved the ichthyosaurs in the Holzmaden quarries were also very successful in preserving the marine crocodile *Steneosaurus*. We can see that it was very much like a modern crocodile. Its legs and feet show it to have been an animal that spent much of its time on land. However the occurrence of its fossils at Holzmaden and in marine deposits in England show that it was also a sea-going beast.

The Truth About Sea Creatures

Q: How did *Tylosaurus* move through the water?

Tylosaurus had joined toes that formed a paddle. It used its flat tail to push itself through the water with powerful sideways strokes.

Q: Could *Elasmosaurus* breathe underwater?

A: *Elasmosaurus* had tiny nostrils, but they were not used for breathing. They helped sense prey moving in the water. To breathe, *Elasmosaurus* came to the surface and breathed through its mouth.

Q: How did elasmosaurs hunt for food?

A: An elasmosaur is a type of plesiosaur with a very long neck. It is thought that such creatures swam directly under the waves and reached down with their long necks to catch fish. Having such a long neck enabled the elasmosaur to keep its body out of sight, so that it could sneak up on unexpecting prey.

Q: Why are most of the fossils ever found those of sea-living animals?

A: Fossils are found in sedimentary rocks, and these are usually formed from mud and sand laid down unter water. Sea animals are more likely to be buried in the seabed and become fossils when the sediments eventually turn to rock.

Q: Did ancient sea creatures lay eggs?

A: Not all of them. Although many ancient reptiles laid eggs, some gave birth to live young. *Ichthyosaurus*, which looked a bit like a shark or a dolphin, gave birth to its young underwater, and fossils have even been found that show this.

Q: Why did *Cryptoclidus* have such spiky teeth?

Cryptoclidus ate squid and fish. It had long, pointed teeth so that it could snatch up its slippery prey without it getting away.

Q: Why is it that stomach stones have been found in the fossilized skeletons of pliosaurs?

A: Sea-living animals, like *Liopleurodon*, swallowed stones to help adjust their weight and help them sink in the water; to surface, the creature would spit them out again. This lighter weight, plus *Liopleurodon's* streamlined body made it very quick and its massive jaws gave it a bite stronger than *Tyrannosaurus rex*.

Q: How big was *Kronosaurus*?

A: An adult *Kronosaurus* grew up to 10 metres (35 ft) long and could weigh as much as 20 tonnes. It was so big and such a fierce predator that it had no competition in the water. It is thought that this creature lurked in deep, deep waters, as very few fossils have been found. Because of this, very little is known about *Kronosaurus*, such as how it reproduced.

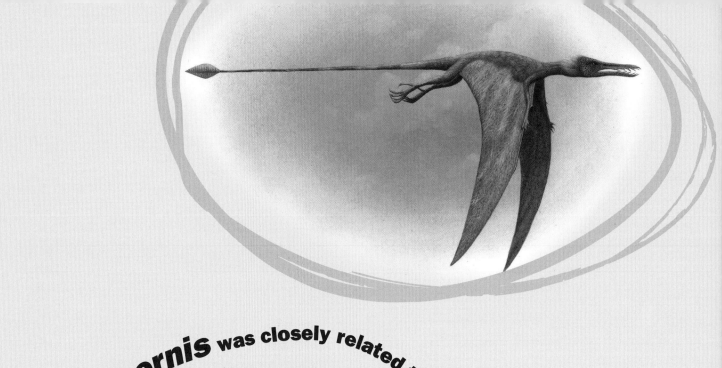

Bullockornis was closely related to modern ducks.

Chapter 4:
In the Sky

Just as the ancient
Earth and its oceans teemed with
reptiles of all kinds so, too, did the sky.
Numerous **wonderful creatures** developed
flight during the Reptile Age – some of them closely
related to dinosaurs, if not dinosaurs in their own right. Which
were the early **flying reptiles?** Who discovered the
first pterosaur? How did these flying creatures get about when
walking? And did some of them have **feathers?** Since the
discovery of *Archaeopteryx*, thought to be **half bird-half
dinosaur**, scientists have made many discoveries about
the beasts that took to the skies all those millions of
years ago. Delve into this chapter to learn about
this **amazing** world for yourself.

The Pioneers

While the dinosaurs, fish and mammals were colonizing the land and the sea during prehistoric times, the sky up above was buzzing with activity. Early flyers were simple organisms, but nature gradually came up with more complex designs. First came the insects, who continue to flourish today. Next came the flying reptiles, gliding creatures which evolved from ground-living, lizard-like animals. These reptiles were replaced in terms of importance by the pterosaurs, probably the most famous of the ancient flying reptiles. Finally, the first birds appeared halfway through the Age of Dinosaurs, and they have continued to rule the skies to this day.

The First Kings

Meganeura was like a dragonfly, but much larger – the size of a parrot. Its wings were typical insect wings, consisting of a thin sheet of chitin, supported by a network of rigid veins. *Meganeura* lived in Carboniferous times, not long after insects first evolved.

As with flying insects of today, *Meganeura* had four wings.

Wing for Gliding

The earliest flying reptile known was the Permian *Coelurosauravus*. It looked very much like a lizard, but its ribs were extended out to the side and supported gliding wings made of skin. The modern flying lizard of Malaysia glides in exactly the same manner.

Triassic	Early/Mid Jurassic	Late Jurassic	Early Cretaceous	Late Cretaceous
245–208 MYA	208–157 MYA	157–146 MYA	146–97 MYA	97–65 MYA

Amber Perfection

The best fossils come from amber preservation. When an unwary insect gets stuck in the sticky resin that oozes from tree trunks, the resin engulfs the insect and preserves it perfectly. When the tree dies and becomes buried, over a long period of time the resin solidifies and becomes the mineral we call amber. The 1994 film *Jurassic Park* was based on the premise that foreign DNA could be taken from biting insects preserved in amber to recreate the creature that was bitten. While this might not be possible today, it is an exciting concept.

Early Birds

Birds such as this *Sinornis* appeared about halfway through the Age of Dinosaurs, evolving from the dinosaurs themselves. Birds continue to thrive, and are the main flying vertebrates today. Their wings are made of a bony structure consisting of some of the fingers fused together, supporting feathers fanning out from the arms.

Pterosaurs were the largest creatures ever to fly.

King of the Skies

Gliders like *Coelurosauravus* were replaced in importance by the pterosaurs by late Triassic times. These famous flying reptiles were the first vertebrates to adapt to a life of active flight. They appeared at about the same time as the first dinosaurs, and became extinct at the end of the Cretaceous period. Pterosaur wings were made of reinforced skin stretched out on an arm and an elongated fourth finger.

Early Flying Reptiles

The simplest kind of flight is a gliding flight – one that needs little in the way of muscular effort. All that is required is a lightness of body, and some kind of aerofoil structure that catches the air and allows the body to be carried along upon it, like a paper dart. In modern times we see this in flying squirrels and flying lizards. There were a number of flying reptiles in Permian and Triassic times, and each one evolved independently from different reptile ancestors.

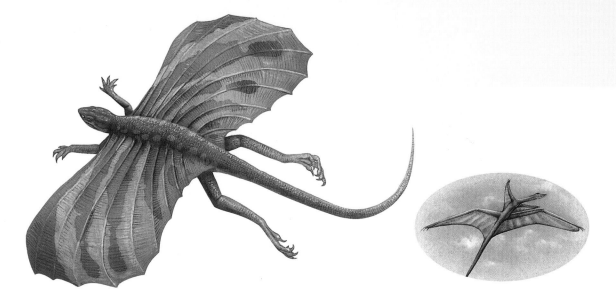

A Famous Find

A famous specimen of late Triassic *Icarosaurus* was discovered by a schoolboy in New Jersey, USA. The partial skeleton shows it to have been a lizard-like animal with long projections from its ribs. The angles at which the rib extensions lay suggested that the wings could have been folded back out of the way when the animal was at rest. Several decades after the discovery, the finder realized that under United States law the specimen was his by rights, and it is now lost to science, having disappeared into his private collection.

Sharovipteryx in Flight

When alive, *Sharovipteryx* must have been able to glide using the wings on its hind legs. This would not have been a very stable type of flight, but it was probably efficient enough to transport the reptile from one tree to another. Small skin flaps on the forelimbs would have helped to control the flight. With the wing membrane stretched on elongated limbs, *Sharovipteryx* must have resembled a kind of a back-to-front pterosaur. Indeed it has been suggested that it may have been among the pterosaurs' early relatives.

Permian	Triassic	Early/Mid Jurassic	Late Jurassic	Early Cretaceous
286–248 MYA	245–208 MYA	208–157 MYA	157–146 MYA	146–97 MYA

Longisquama

This is a fossil of the flying reptile *Longisquama*, from late Triassic central Asia. It had a completely different type of flying mechanism. A double row of long scales stuck up along the backbone, each scale forming a shallow V-shape along its mid line. When spread, these would have overlapped like the feathers of a bird to give a continuous gliding surface. Perhaps they were a precursor to the evolution of feathers in birds, which appeared 60 million years later.

Solar Powered

Kuehneosaurus was a gliding reptile that existed in western England in late Triassic times. It was very similar in structure to *Icarosaurus*. There were about a dozen wing supports (about half the number of the earlier *Coelurosauravus*), suggesting that the wings were longer and narrower, and probably more manoeuvrable. The skin of the wings was probably rich in blood vessels and the wings may have been able to warm up the animal in the sun like a solar panel.

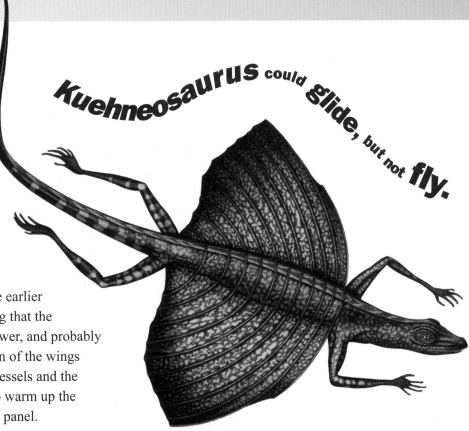

Kuehneosaurus could glide, but not fly.

Long Legs

Late Triassic *Sharovipteryx* from central Asia was a small lizard-like animal about the size of a sparrow, with the most ridiculous-looking hind legs, each one longer than the complete length of the body. These long legs only made sense when it was noticed that there was the imprint of a membrane of skin stretched between them and the middle of the tail.

The Discovery of the Pterosaurs

The first pterosaur fossil to have been scientifically studied was an almost perfect skeleton from the lithographic limestone quarries of Solnhofen in Germany, discovered in 1784. Although the skeleton was just about complete, it was impossible to compare it with any animal alive at the time, so the find remained a mystery. Seventeen years later, the French pioneer naturalist Baron Georges Cuvier guessed that it was a flying animal. Scientists have since come up with many different ideas of what pterosaurs were and how they existed.

Devilish Pterosaurs

In 1840 British geologist Thomas Hawkins published a book on the fossil sea reptiles (the ichthyosaurs and plesiosaurs) that had been discovered up to that time. The frontispiece of the book was an engraving by John Martin, an English painter of biblical and historical subjects. It was a nightmare scene in which he depicted monstrous ichthyosaurs and plesiosaurs and pterosaurs that resembled bat-winged demons.

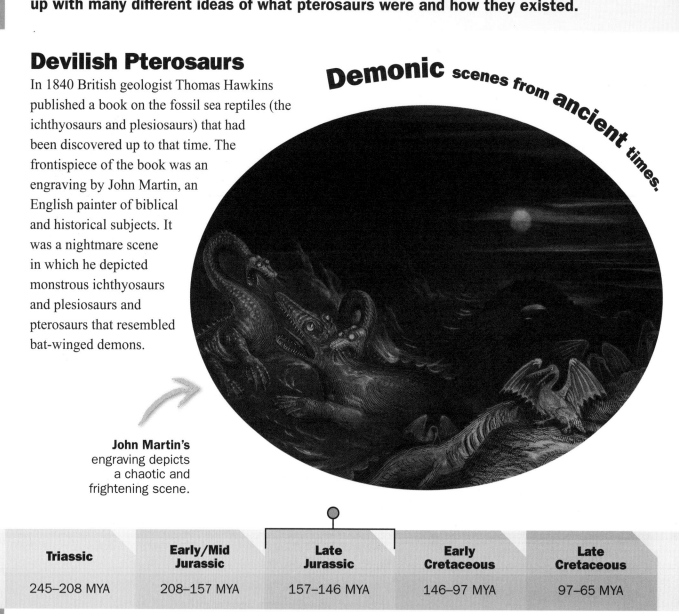

Demonic scenes from ancient times.

John Martin's engraving depicts a chaotic and frightening scene.

Triassic	Early/Mid Jurassic	Late Jurassic	Early Cretaceous	Late Cretaceous
245–208 MYA	208–157 MYA	157–146 MYA	146–97 MYA	97–65 MYA

Jurassic Bats?

English geologist Sir Henry De la Beche produced a drawing in 1830 showing animal life in the Jurassic (then called Liassic) sea of southern England. It consisted of swimming reptiles, fish and ammonites, and in the air there were flying pterosaurs. De la Beche depicted pterosaurs as bat-like creatures, with their wing membranes stretching all the way down to their feet.

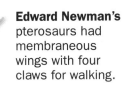

Edward Newman's pterosaurs had membraneous wings with four claws for walking.

Victorian depictions of ancient reptiles tend to be macabre and fanciful. They reflect the Romantic movement that dominated the arts.

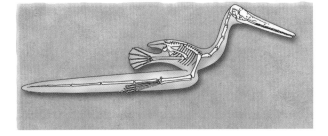

Flying Marsupials

A surprisingly modern interpretation of pterosaurs was drawn in 1843 by Edward Newman. He regarded them as flying marsupials. Although the mouse ears are inaccurate, the furry bodies and the predatory lifestyle are well in-keeping with how we now regard these creatures.

Swimming Pterosaurs

In 1784, the idea was put forward that pterosaurs were not flying animals but swimming animals. This theory influenced many scientists and artists, including Johann Wagler, whose 1830 sketch (left) suggested that pterosaurs were an intermediate stage between mammals and birds.

Pterosaur Paradise

The region of Solnhofen in southern Germany has produced a treasure trove of finds – fossils so good that every detail of even the most delicate of organisms can still be seen. The rock is made of very fine particles and was formed under conditions totally lacking in oxygen, so that no further decay was possible. The technical name that geologists give to such occurrences is *Lagerstätten*. There are only about a dozen such sites known, and most people regard Solnhofen as the best in the world.

Ancient Ocean

Over millions of years the surface of the Earth has changed due to the action of plate tectonics, the name given to the activity that occurs under the Earth's surface. Hot magma rises, forcing the Earth to tear on the surface, separating previously joined landmasses. In late Jurassic times the area of southern Germany, including Solnhofen, lay in the shallows along the northern edge of the Tethys Ocean. This ocean separated Europe from Africa. Nowadays all that is left of the Tethys is the Mediterranean Sea and the drying puddles of the Black Sea, the Caspian Sea and the Aral Sea, all flanked by the mountains that were pushed up out of the Earth as the continents collided.

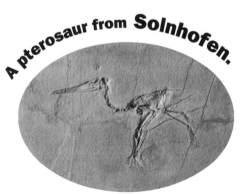

A pterosaur from Solnhofen.

The Modern Quarries

The Romans excavated the fine limestone from Solnhofen to make tiles and paving stones. In the 18th century the fine-grained surface of the rock was found to be ideal for printing, and this led to the rapid expansion of the quarry workings. Despite the fact that these quarries are famous for their fossils, it takes the removal of a vast volume of rock to find one worthwhile skeleton.

Triassic	Early/Mid Jurassic	Late Jurassic	Early Cretaceous	Late Cretaceous
245–208 MYA	208–157 MYA	157–146 MYA	146–97 MYA	97–65 MYA

Anatomy of a Lagoon

Along the edge of the continental shelf to the north of the Tethys Ocean, a vast reef of sponges grew in the deeper waters. As it approached the surface, the reef stopped growing as the sponges died and coral reefs started to grow on top of them. Eventually, a series of lagoons were formed between the reef and the land. Low islands lay across the lagoon, and these (as well as the hinterland) were arid, with only a few scraggly plants. The stagnant water in the lagoon became poisonous and killed any animal that swam or fell into it. Because fine sediment was accumulating below, these animals were preserved almost perfectly.

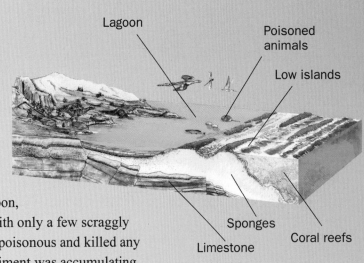

Lagoon

Poisoned animals

Low islands

Sponges

Coral reefs

Limestone

Remains of this reef can now be found stretching from Spain to Romania.

The Headless Ones

Many of the pterosaur fossils found at Solnhofen are without their heads. One possible explanation for this follows.

It is likely that, when the pterosaurs died, they fell into the shallow waters along the northern edge of the Tethys Ocean.

When the pterosaurs landed, because their bodies were so lightweight they floated at the surface for a while.

While lying on the surface, their floating bodies began to decay and their heads, being the heaviest parts, fell off first.

Eventually, after their heads had fallen off, the rest of the pterosaurs' bodies sank to the lagoon floor, where they were quickly covered in fine sediment.

The Earliest Pterosaur

The pterosaurs were the most important of the flying animals in Triassic, Jurassic and Cretaceous times. Once they evolved, they quickly adopted all the features that were to remain with the group for the rest of their existence. Pterosaurs fall into two groups. The more primitive group – the rhamphorhynchoids – had long tails, short wrist bones and narrow wings. These were the first to evolve, appearing in Triassic times. The other group – the pterodactyloids – evolved later, towards the end of the Jurassic.

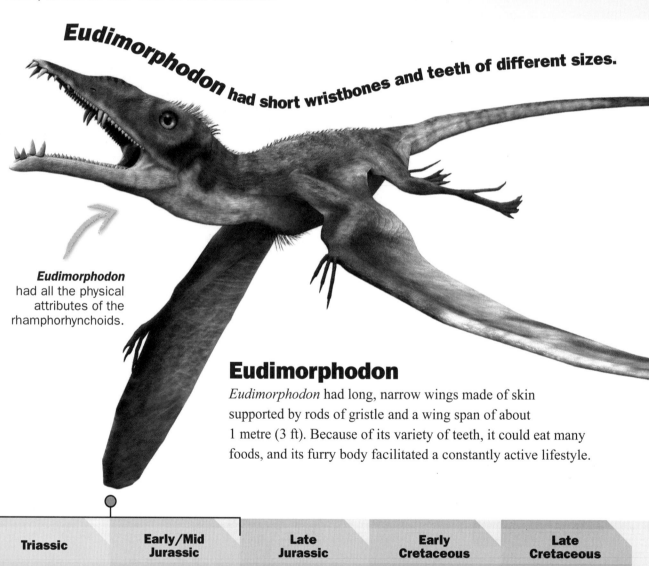

Eudimorphodon had short wristbones and teeth of different sizes.

Eudimorphodon had all the physical attributes of the rhamphorhynchoids.

Eudimorphodon

Eudimorphodon had long, narrow wings made of skin supported by rods of gristle and a wing span of about 1 metre (3 ft). Because of its variety of teeth, it could eat many foods, and its furry body facilitated a constantly active lifestyle.

Triassic	Early/Mid Jurassic	Late Jurassic	Early Cretaceous	Late Cretaceous
245–208 MYA	208–157 MYA	157–146 MYA	146–97 MYA	97–65 MYA

An Educated Guess

Two good fossils of *Eudimorphodon* are known. They both have the wings folded to the body but the wing membrane has not been preserved. Nor is there any direct evidence of a furry pelt. We can, however, guess what the membrane and the fur were like by comparing the fossils with other better preserved pterosaurs.

A modern-day zebra finch in flight.

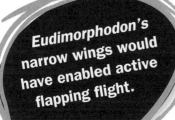

Eudimorphodon's narrow wings would have enabled active flapping flight.

Wing Muscles

The pterosaurs must have had a flying action like modern bats or birds. The arrangement of the shoulder bones and the wing bones show that the muscles present facilitated active flapping flight.

Catching Prey

Many pterosaurs caught fish and, judging by its teeth, *Eudimorphodon* was one of them. The balance of the animal in flight was so delicate that it would not have been able to fly with a fish in its mouth. The pterosaur would have had to have swallowed the fish immediately to get it to its centre of balance.

Big Heads

Rhamphorhynchoid pterosaurs ruled the skies during the early Jurassic period. The earliest Jurassic pterosaur known was discovered in 1828 by the famous professional collector Mary Anning. It was given the name *Dimorphodon* because of its two types of teeth. At 35 centimetres (14 in) tall, it may not have been particularly big, but it was probably the largest pterosaur of its time. Even today, scientists are still in disagreement over many of its features – how it moved around on the ground, for example. These disagreements are typical of our lack of knowledge of the pterosaurs in general.

The rhamphorhynchoid, *Dimorphodon*, had a wingspan of 1.2 metres (4 ft).

Jurassic Skies

Above the early Jurassic shorelines the air was thick with wheeling pterosaurs. They were all of the long-tailed rhamphorhynchoid type. Within a few million years these would all have been replaced by a new pterosaur group – the short-tailed, long-necked, long-wristed pterodactyloids.

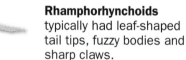

Rhamphorhynchoids typically had leaf-shaped tail tips, fuzzy bodies and sharp claws.

Triassic	Early/Mid Jurassic	Late Jurassic	Early Cretaceous	Late Cretaceous
245–208 MYA	208–157 MYA	157–146 MYA	146–97 MYA	97–65 MYA

Dimorphodon Skeleton

The skeletons of *Dimorphodon* fall to pieces and are crushed easily, because they are made up of the finest struts of bone. Nevertheless there have been two good specimens found, and both of these are in the Natural History Museum in London, England.

It is possible that *Dimorphodon*, and pterosaurs like it, walked on all fours.

On the Ground

We know that pterosaurs like *Dimorphodon* were very adept at flight, but we are not sure of how they moved around when they were not flying. The old theory was that pterosaurs crawled like lizards, while some scientists saw them as running on their hind legs like birds, with their wings folded out of the way. However, footprints in lake sediments from South America attributed to pterosaurs show the marks of the hind feet walking in a narrow track, with marks seemingly made by the claws of the forelimbs in a wider track on each side. This suggests that pterosaurs were walking upright, using the arms like crutches or walking sticks.

Brilliant Beak

Dimorphodon had two different types of teeth – good for grabbing and holding on to slippery prey such as fish. The skull was very high and narrow, and consisted of windows separated by fine struts of bone. It is very likely that the sides of the head were brightly coloured for signalling, just like the beaks of modern tall-beaked birds such as puffins or toucans.

Soft Coverings

Most fossils are of sea-living animals, because sea-living animals have a better chance of falling to the seabed and eventually becoming entombed in sedimentary rock. However, many pterosaurs lived in coastal areas or around lakes, and fell into the water when they died. Sometimes they were fossilized in environments that preserved the finest of details, such as wing membranes and furry coverings.

Furry Pterosaur

The fossil of the rhamphorhynchoid *Sordes*, discovered among late Jurassic lake deposits in Kazakhstan in 1971, proved what many palaeontologists had thought for a long time – that the pterosaurs were covered in hair. The sediment was so fine and the fossilization so complete that not only was the wing membrane preserved, but fibrous patches were visible on the whole of the body, except for the tail.

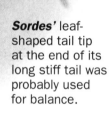

Sordes' leaf-shaped tail tip at the end of its long stiff tail was probably used for balance.

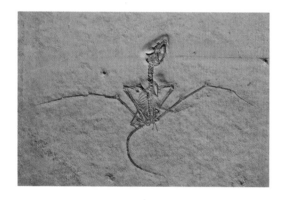

The Best Preserved

This *Rhamphorhynchus* from the Solnhofen deposits in Germany is one of the best preserved pterosaur fossils we have. Even the structure of its wing membrane is visible.

Triassic	Early/Mid Jurassic	Late Jurassic	Early Cretaceous	Late Cretaceous
245–208 MYA	208–157 MYA	157–146 MYA	146–97 MYA	97–65 MYA

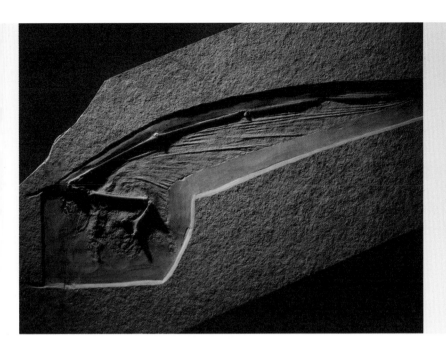

Wing Structure

The wing membrane of a pterosaur was stiffened by fine rods of gristle that fanned out from the arm and hand to the wing's trailing edge. The pattern of the gristle stiffening is the same as the arrangement of the flight feathers of a bird, and the supporting fingers of a bat's wing.

A modern-day bat stretches its **membraneous** wings in flight.

Membraneous wings and a furry body give the bat much in common with the ancient pterosaurs.

How Were the Wings Attached?

There is a great deal of uncertainty about just how the pterosaur's wings were attached to the animal. Some scientists think that the wings stretched from the arms and fourth finger to the body, and did not touch the hind limbs (left). Perhaps they were attached to the hind limbs at the knee (centre). Alternatively, it is quite possible that the wings stretched right down to the ankle (right).

A Modern Interpretation?

It is often thought that birds are the modern equivalent of the pterosaurs. However the modern bat has more in common with the pterosaur than any bird. Pterosaurs and birds shared the Cretaceous skies, but bats did not evolve until pterosaurs died out. This in itself seems to suggest that bats rather than birds occupy the pterosaurs' niche in modern times.

The Most Famous

It is *Pterodactylus* that gives the pterodactyloid group its name, and indeed pterosaurs are commonly referred to as 'pterodactyls'. The pterodactyloids dominated in late Jurassic times, but there have been several different types found dating from this time, so scientists believe that their evolution must have been under way somewhat earlier.

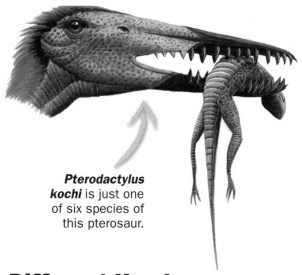

Pterodactylus kochi is just one of six species of this pterosaur.

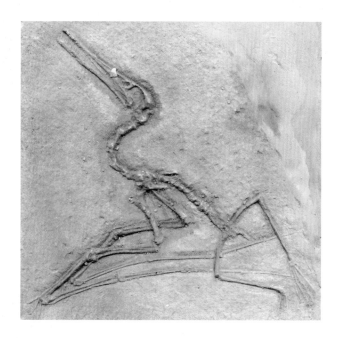

Different Heads, Different Hoods

There were a number of different species of *Pterodactylus*, each one adapted for a particular lifestyle and for eating a particular food. The smaller species with the tiny teeth were probably insect-eaters, while the bigger forms would probably have eaten fish or small lizards. A total of six species are currently acknowledged, all discovered in Solnhofen, Germany. We used to think that there were far more, but many of these finds have subsequently turned out to be juveniles of the already known species.

Pterodactylus Fossil

As with *Rhamphorhynchus*, the best specimens of *Pterodactylus* have been found in the limestone deposits of Solnhofen. They clearly show the details of the skeleton and occasionally the imprints of the wing membranes. Sometimes there is even the imprint of a throat pouch rather like that of a pelican. Other remains of *Pterodactylus* have been found in similar-aged rocks on the south coast of England and in dinosaur-rich deposits in Tanzania.

Triassic	Early/Mid Jurassic	Late Jurassic	Early Cretaceous	Late Cretaceous
245–208 MYA	208–157 MYA	157–146 MYA	146–97 MYA	97–65 MYA

Theory of Evolution

When the British scientist Charles Darwin visited the Galapagos islands in the 19th century, he was struck by the fact that there were a variety of different beak shapes among one family of finch. Their beak shape supported their different lifestyles – heavy beaks for cracking seeds and short beaks for pecking insects and so on. This revelation triggered Darwin's theory of evolution – the idea that over millions of years, creatures could evolve to adapt to their surroundings. The variation in shape of the heads of the various *Pterodactylus* species fits in perfectly with Darwin's theory.

Pterodactyluses have longer heads and necks than species of rhamphorhynchoid tend to have.

Pterodactylus in Flight

There is little doubt that the pterodactyloids originally evolved from the rhamphorhynchoids, but *Pterodactylus* does have several differences from the group. The neck vertebrae in a *Pterodactylus* are particularly long. The head meets the neck at a right angle, rather than being in a straight line, and its skull is more lightly-built. *Pterodactylus* has a short tail, with no steering or flying function, and its long wrist bones mean that the three fingers of the 'hand' are further down the wing.

Heads & Crests

There are birds of every kind today, ranging from perching birds and swimming birds to wading birds and hunting birds. Modern birds have a variety of different heads and beaks – deep, strong beaks for cracking nuts; long, pointed beaks for probing mud; short, sharp beaks for pecking insects; and hooked beaks for tearing flesh. This variety was just as pronounced among the pterodactyloids. As the Age of Reptiles continued, they diversified into all different types, and had different head shapes to suit their different lifestyles.

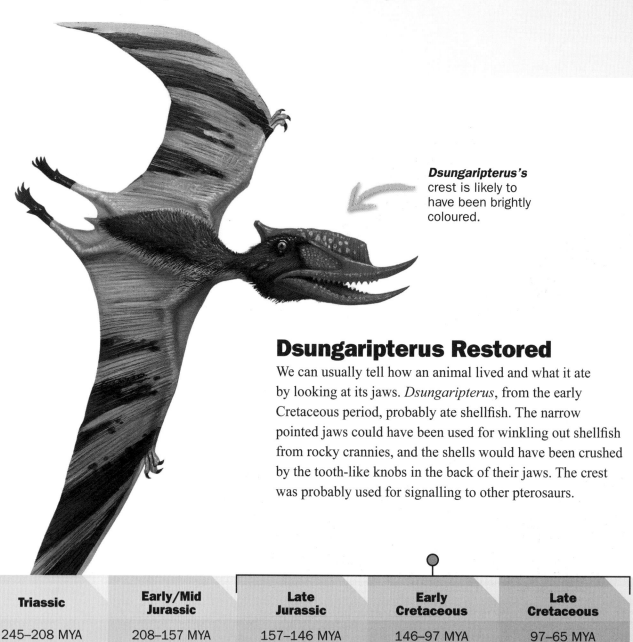

Dsungaripterus's crest is likely to have been brightly coloured.

Dsungaripterus Restored

We can usually tell how an animal lived and what it ate by looking at its jaws. *Dsungaripterus*, from the early Cretaceous period, probably ate shellfish. The narrow pointed jaws could have been used for winkling out shellfish from rocky crannies, and the shells would have been crushed by the tooth-like knobs in the back of their jaws. The crest was probably used for signalling to other pterosaurs.

Triassic	Early/Mid Jurassic	Late Jurassic	Early Cretaceous	Late Cretaceous
245–208 MYA	208–157 MYA	157–146 MYA	146–97 MYA	97–65 MYA

Hideous Find

One of the most grotesque of the pterosaurs was *Dsungaripterus*. It had a beak like a pair of upturned forceps, a battery of crushing, tooth-like, bony knobs at the back of the jaws and a crest that stretched from the back of the head to the snout. It was a large pterosaur with a wingspan of over 3 metres (10 ft) wide.

Dsungaripterus was the first pterosaur to have been discovered in China.

A Question of Crests

Many pterosaurs had spectacular crests that allowed them to signal to one another and to enable them to identify members of their own species.

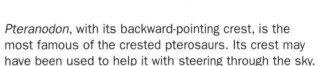

Pteranodon, with its backward-pointing crest, is the most famous of the crested pterosaurs. Its crest may have been used to help it with steering through the sky.

Tupuxuara had a crest that consisted of a vast plate of bone reaching up and beyond the back of the skull. It was full of blood vessels and so it must have been covered in skin. Perhaps it had a heat-regulating function as well as being used for display.

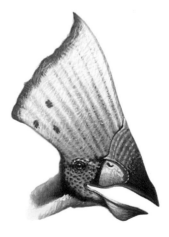

Tapejara was characterized by a tall, bony crest at the front of its skull, probably supporting a flap of skin behind.

The Biggest

Pteranodon was discovered in the 1870s in the late Cretaceous beds of Kansas in the United States. It had a wingspan of over 9 metres (30 ft). Science was astounded, since this was before the development of powered aviation and nobody had really experimented with the sizes of flying structures. Now it looks pretty modest when compared with some more recent discoveries.

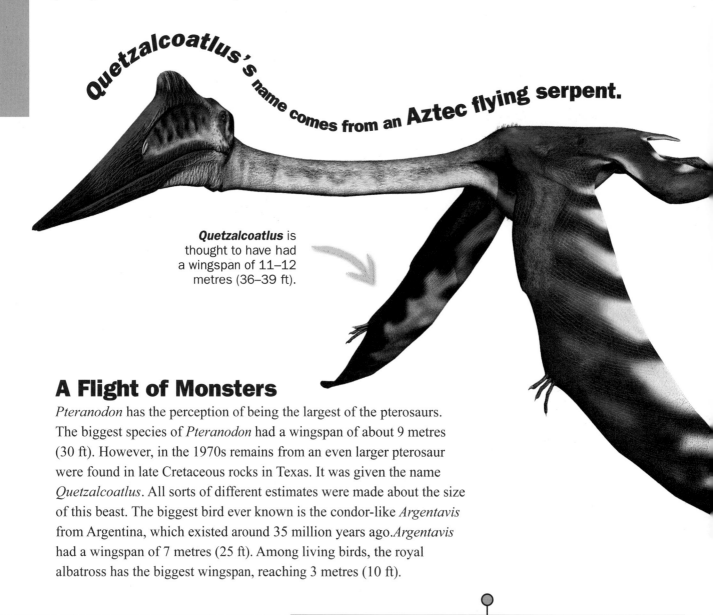

Quetzalcoatlus's name comes from an **Aztec flying serpent.**

Quetzalcoatlus is thought to have had a wingspan of 11–12 metres (36–39 ft).

A Flight of Monsters

Pteranodon has the perception of being the largest of the pterosaurs. The biggest species of *Pteranodon* had a wingspan of about 9 metres (30 ft). However, in the 1970s remains from an even larger pterosaur were found in late Cretaceous rocks in Texas. It was given the name *Quetzalcoatlus*. All sorts of different estimates were made about the size of this beast. The biggest bird ever known is the condor-like *Argentavis* from Argentina, which existed around 35 million years ago. *Argentavis* had a wingspan of 7 metres (25 ft). Among living birds, the royal albatross has the biggest wingspan, reaching 3 metres (10 ft).

Triassic	Early/Mid Jurassic	Late Jurassic	Early Cretaceous	Late Cretaceous
245–208 MYA	208–157 MYA	157–146 MYA	146–97 MYA	97–65 MYA

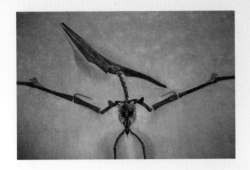

Pteranodon Skeleton

This partial skeleton of the giant pterosaur *Pteranodon* was found in Cretaceous rocks in Kansas, USA. It shows a skull fragment, the bones of the wing finger and the complete hind legs. The whole skeleton was extremely lightweight, and the bones had openings to allow the penetration of air sacks, connected to the lungs. This system is seen in modern birds.

As many as 1,200 *Pteranodon* fossils have been discovered – more than those of any other pterasaur.

The Biggest

The current record holder is *Arambourgiania*, a pterodactyloid that may have had a wingspan of about 12 metres (39 ft). It had an extremely long neck, and when the neck bones were first found they were thought to have been the long finger bones that supported the wing. The original name given to it was *Titanopteryx*, but that name had already been given to something else, so the title had to be changed.

The Smallest

At the other end of the scale, the tiny pterosaur *Anurognathus* holds the record for the smallest pterosaur known. It had a wingspan of about 50 cm (2 ft). Its short head contained little peg-like teeth, ideal for catching and crushing insects. Despite its short pterodactyloid-like tail, it is actually a member of the more primitive rhamphorhynchoids. Only one skeleton has been found, and that was in the late Jurassic Solnhofen deposits.

The First Bird

In 1859 Charles Darwin published *The Origin of Species*, creating an immediate sensation. How could animals have evolved into different types over a long period if they had all been created at the same time, as it says in the Bible? The scientific community found itself in opposition to the overpowering influence of traditional biblical teaching. Then, two years later, a remarkable fossil was discovered in the quarries of Solnhofen. It was obviously a dinosaur, but it sported bird's wings and was covered in feathers. Here were the remains of a creature that appeared to be a stage in the evolution of birds from dinosaurs. Today, few scientists dispute the notion that *Archaeopteryx* (as this creature was named) evolved from dinosaur ancestors.

The Living Archaeopteryx

Had we seen *Archaeopteryx* in life, fluttering away from us, there would be no doubt in our minds that we were looking at a bird, albeit a rather clumsy one. However, a closer look would reveal a set of toothed jaws, just like a dinosaur, instead of the usual bird beak. The tail appeared to be paddle-shaped, unlike a modern bird's muscular stump with a bunch of feathers. This tail was a stiff straight rod, like a dinosaur's tail, with feathers growing from each side. The final oddity would be the claws, three of them protruding from the leading edge of the wing.

Solnhofen fossil finds suggested that *Archaeopteryx* was part bird, part dinosaur.

Triassic	Early/Mid Jurassic	Late Jurassic	Early Cretaceous	Late Cretaceous
245–208 MYA	208–157 MYA	157–146 MYA	146–97 MYA	97–65 MYA

Vindicating Darwin

Eight *Archaeopteryx* fossils have been found so far, all from the Solnhofen quarries, ranging in quality from a single feather to an almost complete bony skeleton with feathers. One was found in a private collection, having been misidentified as the small dinosaur *Compsognathus*. This specimen did not show the feathers, and the misidentification serves to emphasize the resemblance between the primitive bird and the dinosaur ancestor.

Characteristics seen in the *Archaeopteryx* feather are identical to those of modern birds.

Feather

The first *Archaeopteryx* fossil to be found was a perfectly conventional flight feather. The main support is a vane that is off-centre, showing that it is from a wing and used for flight. The filaments forming the vane of the feather had rows of hooks that enabled them to fix to one another to give stability. There was a downy portion at the base for insulation

The Wing

The wing of *Archaeopteryx* was no halfway measure. Apart from the clawed fingers, it was identical in structure to the wing of a modern flying bird, with the elongated finger-like primary feathers, bunched secondaries and coverts streamlining the whole structure. The wing muscles would have been weaker than those of a modern bird as there was no strong keeled breastbone to anchor them, but the flying action must have been the same.

Chinese 'Gang of Three'

Across the contemporary European-Asian landmass, where China's Liaoning province now lies, a series of forest-shrouded inland lakes produced fossils that were just as spectacular as those from Solnhofen. These include three kinds of animal that, like *Archaeopteryx*, show the evolutionary connection between birds and dinosaurs. Only recently, with improved scientific exchanges between China and the West, is their true significance being fully appreciated.

Caudipteryx's Environment

Caudipteryx, part of the Chinese 'Gang of Three', lived in an environment like the one shown here. Forests of conifers and ginkgoes, with an undergrowth of ferns and cycads, provided refuge and food for all sorts of different animals in late Jurassic and early Cretaceous China. Lizards and small mammals scampered through the undergrowth and little feathered theropod dinosaurs hunted between the trees. The air was colonized by birds (some looking rather like modern types), while on the ground raced several different half-dinosaur, half-bird creatures.

Caudipteryx watches two dinosaurs approach.

Early Cretaceous
China, with its forests of lush undergrowth.

Triassic	Early/Mid Jurassic	Late Jurassic	Early Cretaceous	Late Cretaceous
245–208 MYA	208–157 MYA	157–146 MYA	146–97 MYA	97–65 MYA

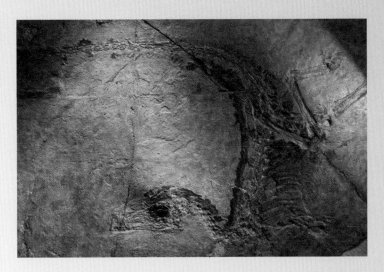

Sinosauropteryx Fossil

The downy covering on some skeletons shows *Sinosauropteryx* to have been related to the birds. Apart from that, it is pure meat-eating dinosaur. The long legs and tail show it to have been a swift-running animal, while the short arms were armed with three claws. From their stomach contents, the skeletons of *Sinosauropteryx* that have been found show that they hunted lizards and small mammals that existed at that time.

Half-Bird, Half-Dinosaur

Another small animal was *Protarchaeopteryx*. It was about the same size as *Sinosauropteryx* but it had a short tail and much longer arms. It was also covered in fuzz and, although the only skeleton found was very jumbled up, there seemed to be long feathers along the arms and tail. The feathers on the arms would have given a wing-like structure.

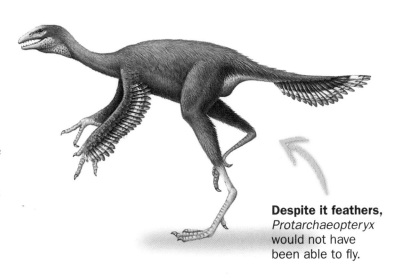

Despite it feathers, *Protarchaeopteryx* would not have been able to fly.

Three skeletons of *Sinosauripteryx* have been found in all.

The meat-eating dromaeosaurids (see page 28) have always been recognized as being very birdlike.

Sinosauripteryx

One of the little dinosaurs present in the Liaoning province was *Sinosauropteryx*. It seems to have been covered in fur or feathers. The preservation is so good that a kind of downy fuzz is visible all around the bones. Although there is still some dissent, most scientists are convinced that this represents a covering of 'protofeathers', structures that are part way between hair, like that of a mammal, and feathers, like those of a bird.

Towards Modern Birds

For all its fine feathers, *Archaeopteryx* was still mostly dinosaur. It had a long reptilian tail, fingers on the wings and a jaw full of teeth. Modern birds have stumpy tails called pygostyles, supporting long feathers. Their wing fingers have completely disappeared, and they also have beaks instead of jaws and teeth. These are all weight-saving adaptations, evolved to make the bird as light as possible so that it can fly more efficiently. These features seem to have appeared at different times during the Age of Dinosaurs.

The First Beak

Confuciusornis is the first beaked bird that we know of. A beak is a much more practical, lightweight alternative to the heavy teeth and jaws of a reptile. It consists of a sliver of bone, sheathed in a lightweight horny substance that combines strength with lightness. Anything that reduces their weight is an advantage to a flying animal.

A Modern Tail

Iberomesornis, a fossil bird from early Cretaceous rocks in Spain, is the earliest bird known to have a pygostyle tail. This structure consists of a muscular stump from which the tail feathers grow in a fan arrangement. The muscles of the pygostyle can spread the tail feathers out or bunch them together, helping to control flight or make a display for courting purposes.

Triassic	Early/Mid Jurassic	Late Jurassic	Early Cretaceous	Late Cretaceous
245–208 MYA	208–157 MYA	157–146 MYA	146–97 MYA	97–65 MYA

Flight Control

Eoalulavis from early Cretaceous lake deposits in Spain is the first bird that we know to have carried an alula. This is a tuft of feathers on the leading edge of the wing, more-or-less where our thumb is. With very small movements of this structure the passage of air over the wing can be altered considerably, and this makes the flight much more controllable. All modern birds have this. However, fossils of *Eoalulavis* are unclear about whether or not the bird had other advanced features such as a beak or a pygostyle.

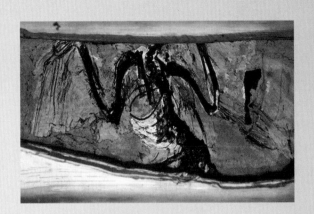

Confuciusornis
Many hundreds of fossils of this creature have been found.

Confuciusornis

Some of the fossils of *Confuciusornis* that have been uncovered at the Liaoning are so well preserved that the details of the plumage are clear. Some have long tail feathers, like those of a bird of paradise, while others have none. This suggests that, as in modern birds, the male species had much more flamboyant plumage than the females.

The Perching Foot

Birds that live in trees usually have feet in which the first toe is turned backwards, enabling the foot to grasp a small branch so the bird can perch. An early example of a perching foot is found in *Changchengornis* – a close relative of *Confuciusornis* – also found in the Liaoning rocks in China. This bird also had a hooked beak, suggesting that it was a meat-eater like a hawk.

Abandoning Flight

It is a fact, that no sooner has a feature evolved, than there are certain lines of evolution that abandon it. As soon as flight evolved, some birds reverted to living on the ground. There are several explanations for this. Perhaps flightless birds evolved in areas where there were no dangerous predators on the ground and so there was no need to fly, or perhaps food was more plentiful on the ground.

Modern-day flightless birds include ostriches, emus and rheas.

Killer Duck

Bullockornis lived in Australia around 20 million years ago. It stood 3 metres (10 ft) high and had a huge beak that was either used for cracking nuts or tearing flesh. An enlarged brain capacity suggests that the latter was more likely, as quick senses are necessary for hunting down prey. It was unrelated to the emus or the cassowaries, or any other type of flightless bird that exists in Australia today. Despite its dinosaur-like appearance, *Bullockornis* was actually a kind of a duck.

The duck-like *Bullockornis* stood 3 metres (10 ft) tall.

Early Cretaceous	Late Cretaceous	Paleogene	Neogene	Quarternary
146–97 MYA	97–65 MYA	65–23 MYA	23–1.8 MYA	1.8–0.01 MYA

The Dinosaur Re-evolved?

Once the dinosaurs died out, a number of huge, flightless hunting birds evolved around 65 million years ago. *Phorusrhachos* of South America and *Diatryma* of North America were built along the lines of medium-sized meat-eating dinosaurs, with fast hind legs and fierce heads. *Titanis* (pictured) from Florida even had tiny clawed hands on the remains of its wings. It is almost as if there had still been a niche for dinosaur-shaped hunting creatures and evolution had filled it with giant hunting birds.

It is thought that *Titanis* would have had strong middle toes.

Dead as a Dodo

Probably the best known of the extinct flightless birds is *Raphus*, the dodo. It evolved from pigeon stock into a ground-dwelling plant-eater on the island of Mauritius. It survived there happily for thousands of years, as there were no ground-living predators. Everything changed, however, when humans arrived on the island, and the bird was wiped out within a few years.

The tallest moas reached 3.6 metres (12 ft) in height.

Plant-eaters

Not only were the shapes of the meat-eating dinosaurs reflected in some of the later birds, but there seemed to be bird versions of the long-necked plant-eaters as well. *Dinornis*, the moa, existed in New Zealand right up until modern times. It thrived there because there were no ground-living predators in New Zealand – until human beings came along and caused its extinction.

Extinction

Although no one can be certain how, or why, dinosaurs died, they became extinct around 65 million years ago. Most scientists believe that, around this time, the Earth was hit by a giant meteorite that landed in present-day Mexico. The damage caused killed off most of the big animals at the time, and this included the dinosaurs.

The explosion would have sent debris over North America, **killing everything** there first.

The rest of the world was affected by an **enormous cloud of dust** that spread out from the impact zone.

A **tsunami** caused by the impact swept 180 miles (300 km) inland across southern North America.

It would have taken **tens of thousands of years** for the effects to have been fully felt, but this is a long time in geological terms.

The Truth About Flight

Q: Were pterosaurs brightly coloured?

A: Scientists think that many of the pterosaurs had striking markings, particularly those that had crests, like this *Tapejara*, and that they used the crests to send signals to one another.

Q: Could any dinosaurs fly?

A: There weren't any true dinosaurs that could fly, although *Microraptor* could glide from tree to tree. When people talk about flying dinosaurs, they usually mean the pterosaurs that took to the skies around the same time.

Q: Did pterosaurs have feathers, like birds?

A: No, they didn't. Instead their bodies were cover in fur and their wings were made of skin that stretched between their front and hind limbs. Some fossils of pterosaurs are so well preserved that you can see small patches of fur still there.

Q: Did insects evolve from dinosaurs

A: Insects did not evolve from dinosaurs, but they have been around for a very long time. They appeared nearly 400 million years ago, during the since the Carboniferous era, and immediately evolved flying types. Few died out in the end-Cretaceous mass extinction, and they are now far more diverse than any other group of creatures. Wings are the tough parts of an insect's anatomy, and it is mostly wings that have been fossilized.

Q: Where did the *Pteranodons* live?

A: *Pteranodon* fossils have been found across North America, notably in Kansas, Nebraska, Alabama, Dakota and Wyoming.

Q: What was the first bird?

A: *Archeopteryx* was the first bird and almost certainly evolved from a dinosaur. While it had feathers like a bird, *Archeopteryx* also had sharp teeth and claws, just like a dinosaur.

Q: Were birds wiped out by the mass extinction

A: The birds lost only three-quarters of their species and those that survived the mass extinction went on to become the true masters of the skies. The birds of today mostly fly, but they can also perch, wade, swim and even burrow. *Presbyornis* was a long-legged wading duck that lived in huge flocks in North America around 65 million years ago. Although it had webbed feet, its legs would have been too long to allow it to swim. The webs probably developed to prevent the bird from sinking into the mud.

Q: How heavy was *Quetzalcoatlus*?

A: *Quetzalcoatlus* was huge – some scientists say it had a wingspan to match that of a small aeroplane, and yet scientists think it weighed as little as an adult man. It is difficult for them to be accurate about this, howver, because a whole *Quetzalcoatlus* skeleton has not yet been found. All of the work carried out so far has been made on specimens that have been pieced together from different finds.

Kaprosuchus had **massive** tusk-like teeth.

Dinosaur
Fact File

From *Acrocanthosaurus* to *Velociraptor*, and featuring more than **60 ancient creatures** in total, this Fact File presents each dinosaur, marine reptile or flying reptile in turn, together with all of its **vital statistics**. Learn how to say each reptile's name and what it means. Find out **how big** these creatures were and how much they weighed. And discover the special features that set them apart from others. Every so often you'll come across a **confrontation** between two of the dinosaurs. See how each battle starts and find out **who wins** at the end of the book. It is not always as clear cut as you might think!

Acrocanthosaurus

[*Acrocanthosaurus* means: **High-spined Lizard**]

Acrocanthosaurus was one of the largest theropods of the whole dinosaur age, and would have been a top predator in its environment. **Acrocanthosaurus** may have preyed on sauropods – especially the young injured or elderly – and ornithopods. In North America, **Acrocanthosaurus** bones have been found alongside those of *Sauroposeidon*, showing that these two giants lived, or at least died, in the same area.

? How do you say it?
Acro-can-thow-saw-rus

Dino Fact File

Turn to page 218 to see how *Sauroposeidon* fares in battle against *Acrocanthosaurus*.

Name: *Acrocanthosaurus*
Group: Carcharodontosaurid
Discovered: 1940s (Oklahoma, USA)
Fossils: North America
Period: Early Cretaceous
Height: 6 metres (19.5 ft)
Length: 11.5 metres (38 ft)
Weight: 6,000 kilograms (13,300 lbs)
How it moved: On two legs
Diet: Carnivorous
Prey: Sauropods, ornithopods
Main predator: None
Special features: *Acrocanthosaurus* had tall spines down its backbone

Acrocanthosaurus's *skull was up to 1.2 metres (4 ft) long – the height of an 8-year-old child.*

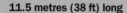

11.5 metres (38 ft) long

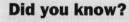

Did you know?

Acrocanthosaurus used its heavy tail to counterbalance the weight of its head and body.

148

Albertasaurus

[*Albertasaurus* means: **Alberta Lizard**]

? **How do you say it?** *Alber-toe-saw-rus*

This tyrannosaur gets its name from the province of Alberta in Canada, where the bones of more than 30 animals have been discovered. The forested landscape, crisscrossed by rivers, would have been a rich hunting ground for this predatory dinosaur. Fossil evidence points to *Albertosaurus* being a pack-hunter – a scary prospect for its potential prey.

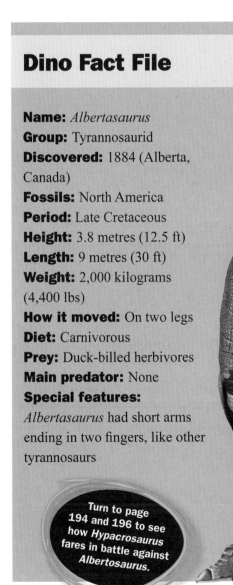

Dino Fact File

Name: *Albertasaurus*
Group: Tyrannosaurid
Discovered: 1884 (Alberta, Canada)
Fossils: North America
Period: Late Cretaceous
Height: 3.8 metres (12.5 ft)
Length: 9 metres (30 ft)
Weight: 2,000 kilograms (4,400 lbs)
How it moved: On two legs
Diet: Carnivorous
Prey: Duck-billed herbivores
Main predator: None
Special features: *Albertasaurus* had short arms ending in two fingers, like other tyrannosaurs

Turn to page 194 and 196 to see how *Hypacrosaurus* fares in battle against *Albertosaurus*.

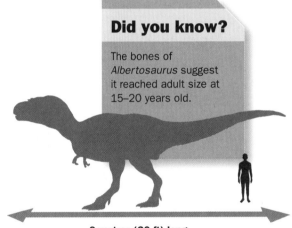

Did you know?

The bones of *Albertosaurus* suggest it reached adult size at 15–20 years old.

9 metres (30 ft) long

Albertasaurus's *jaws were lined with serrated teeth.*

149

Predator Trap

1 The rainy season is long overdue and predators are stalking the last few water holes. **Stegosaurus** approaches a rapidly drying lakebed to drink.

Allosaurus

2 It glances over its shoulder – pushing its head directly into the waiting jaws of **Allosaurus!** Will the bones of this herbivore soon join those of other prey that litter the water holes? Or will it fight back with its powerful tail and killer spikes?

Turn to page 248 to find out.

Stegosaurus

Allosaurus

[*Allosaurus* means: **Different Lizard**]

How do you say it?

Al-oh-saw-rus

The biggest and fiercest meat-eater in the Late Jurassic Period was *Allosaurus*. It was big enough to hunt the largest of the plant-eating sauropods, although it probably concentrated on the young, the old and the injured. After it had finished eating, there would be plenty left over for smaller scavenging dinosaurs and pterosaurs.

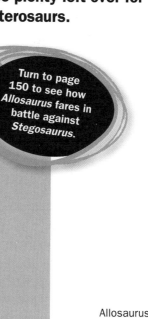

Dino Fact File

Turn to page 150 to see how *Allosaurus* fares in battle against *Stegosaurus*.

Name: *Allosaurus*
Group: Allosaurid
Discovered: 1877 (Colorado, USA)
Fossils: USA, Portugal
Period: Late Jurassic
Height: 5 metres (16.5 ft)
Length: 12 metres (39 ft)
Weight: 5,000 kilograms (11,000 lbs)
How it moved: On two legs
Diet: Carnivorous
Prey: Apatosaurus, Stegosaurus
Main predator: None
Special features: Biggest land-living meat-eater of all time

Allosaurus has small arms and three claws on each hand to grip its prey.

12 metres (39 feet) long

Did you know?

Allosaurus weighed around 5,000 kilos (11,000 lbs) – the weight of an elephant. There were several smaller species, some weighing 1,000 kilos (2,000 lbs), which is still heavy.

Anchisaurus

[*Anchisaurus* means: **Near Lizard**]

? **How do you say it?**
Ank-ee-saw-rus

Anchisaurus is an odd-looking, plant-eating, herbivorous dinosaur. Although this Early Jurassic dinosaur is very small and weighed just 70 kilograms (154 lb), it belongs to the sauropod group, and its descendents would evolve into the largest land animals ever to walk on Earth. It's amazing that these small dinosaurs would give rise to such giants, given their poor diet of fibrous ferns and woody plants.

Dino Fact File

Name: *Anchisaurus*
Group: Sauropod
Discovered: 1818 (Connecticut, USA)
Fossils: Fossils have been found in North America, South Africa and China
Period: Early Jurassic
Height: 1 metre (3.25 ft)
Length: 2 metres (6.5 ft)
Weight: 70 kilograms (154 lbs)
How it moved: On all fours
Diet: Herbivorous
Food: Tough plants and stems
Main predator: *Dilophosaurus*
Special features:
Anchisaurus had to walk on all fours, because of its large tummy

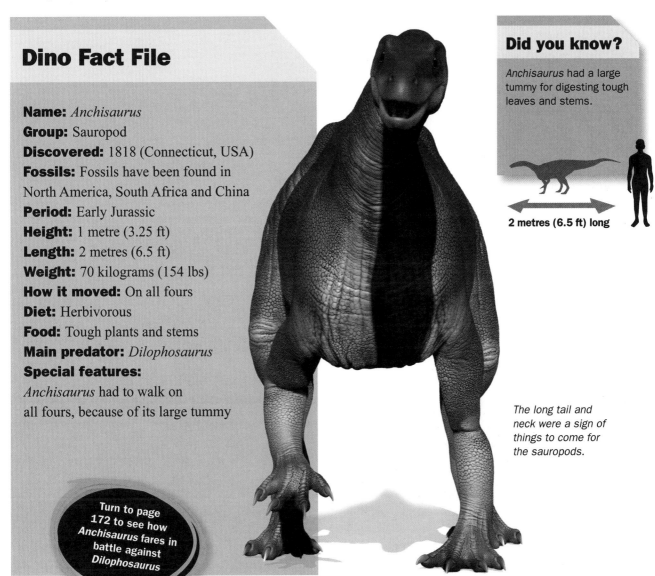

Did you know?

Anchisaurus had a large tummy for digesting tough leaves and stems.

2 metres (6.5 ft) long

The long tail and neck were a sign of things to come for the sauropods.

Turn to page 172 to see how *Anchisaurus* fares in battle against *Dilophosaurus*

Ankylosaurus

[*Ankylosaurus* means: **Fused Lizard**]

? **How do you say it?** *An-key-loh-sawr-us*

Ankylosaurus was the biggest armoured dinosaur that ever lived. But it was a herbivore and needed all the protection it could get from hungry carnivore predators. Its head was a box of solid bone, while its back was covered in hard plates. At the end of ***Ankylosaurus's*** tail was a heavy club – an effective weapon with one swish of the tail.

Dino Fact File

Name: *Ankylosaurus*
Group: Ankylosaurids
Discovered: 1908 (Montana, USA)
Fossils: Western North America
Period: Late Cretaceous Period
Height: 2.5 metres (23 ft)
Length: 7 metres (30 ft)
Weight: 4,000–7,000 kilograms (8,800–15,000 lbs)
How it moved: On all fours
Diet: Herbivorous
Food: Low-lying vegetation
Main predator: *Tyrannosaurus*
Special features: A heavy club on its tail, made from chunks of bone

Did you know?

Ankylosaurus was one of the last dinosaurs standing before extinction.

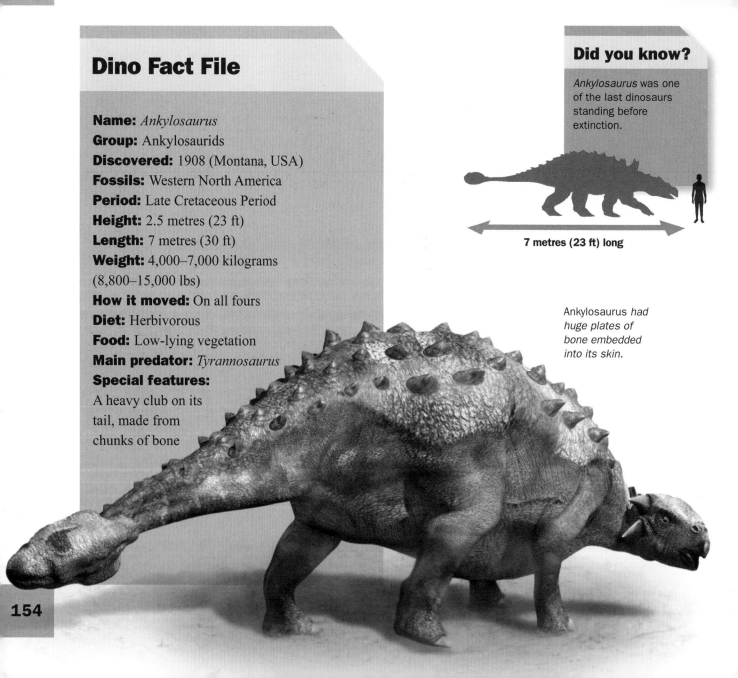

7 metres (23 ft) long

Ankylosaurus *had huge plates of bone embedded into its skin.*

Archaeopteryx

[*Archaeopteryx* means: **Ancient Wing**]

?
How do you say it?
Arc-ee-op-tricks

This small, feathered dinosaur is known as the first bird, but *Archaeopteryx* had features of both a dinosaur and a bird! It has the long, bony tail and toothed jaws of its theropod ancestors but the wishbone and wings of modern birds. *Archaeopteryx* could almost certainly fly, and would have hunted its prey along the shores of the shallow seas and lagoons of Late Jurassic Europe.

Dino Fact File

Turn to page 166 to see how *Archeopteryx* fares in battle against *Compsognathus*.

Name: *Archaeopteryx*
Group: Feathered theropod
Discovered: 1861 (Bavaria, Germany)
Fossils: Europe
Period: Late Jurassic
Height: 30 centimetres (12 in)
Length: 50 centimetres (20 in)
Weight: 0.5 kilograms (1.1 lb)
How it moved: On two legs; gliding
Diet: Carnivorous
Prey: Small animals
Main predator: *Staurikosaurus*
Special features:
Archaeopteryx had sharp, curved claws that helped it to climb or perch

Did you know?

The tips of *Archaeopteryx*'s flight feathers were likely to have been black, while the neck and head probably had no feathers at all.

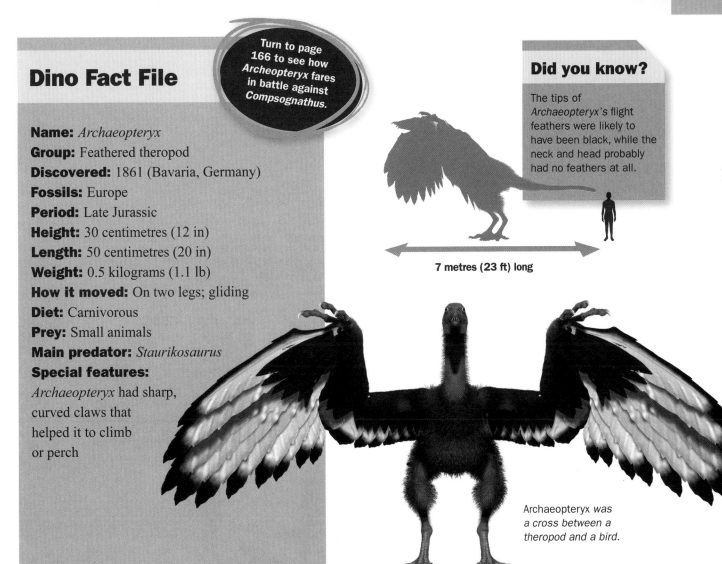

7 metres (23 ft) long

Archaeopteryx was a cross between a theropod and a bird.

Arizonasaurus

[*Arizonasaurus* means: **Lizard from Arizona]**

Arizonasaurus was a kind of crocodile that lived on land, just before the time of the dinosaurs. It lived in the desert and hunted for plant-eating reptiles, like lizards. *Arizonasaurus* had a sail on its back, which scientists think stored heat from the sun. This helped to keep *Arizonasaurus* warm. *Arizonasaurus* didn't crawl like a crocodile, but had straight legs and walked more like a dog.

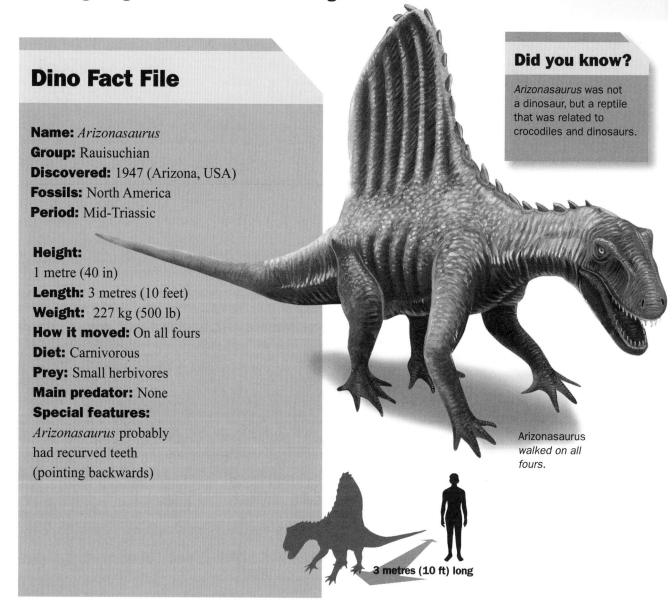

Dino Fact File

Name: *Arizonasaurus*
Group: Rauisuchian
Discovered: 1947 (Arizona, USA)
Fossils: North America
Period: Mid-Triassic

Height:
1 metre (40 in)
Length: 3 metres (10 feet)
Weight: 227 kg (500 lb)
How it moved: On all fours
Diet: Carnivorous
Prey: Small herbivores
Main predator: None
Special features:
Arizonasaurus probably had recurved teeth (pointing backwards)

Did you know?

Arizonasaurus was not a dinosaur, but a reptile that was related to crocodiles and dinosaurs.

Arizonasaurus walked on all fours.

3 metres (10 ft) long

Avaceratops

[*Avaceratops* means: **Ava's Horned Face** **]**

? **How do you say it?** *Av-uh-ser-uh-tops*

Many ceratopsian dinosaurs were discovered over 100 years ago by the first palaeontologists, but this species was not found until 1986. Like all ceratopsian dinosaurs, *Avaceratops* was a herbivore and had a powerful beak. That would cut through foliage. The first ceratopsians were about 1 metre (40 in) long, but later ones, such as *Avaceratops* was as big as a bull.

Dino Fact File

Turn to page 236 to see how Avaceratops fares in battle against Troodon.

Did you know?

Avaceratops's head horns grew to about 25 cm (10 in) long.

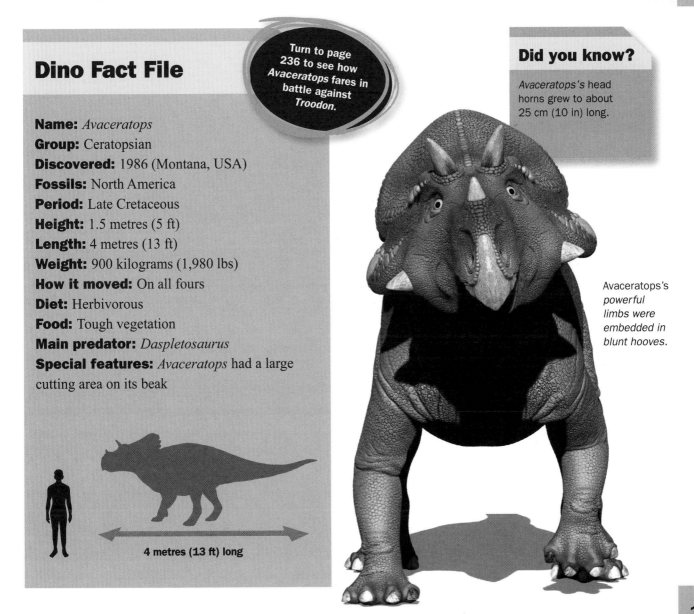

Name: *Avaceratops*
Group: Ceratopsian
Discovered: 1986 (Montana, USA)
Fossils: North America
Period: Late Cretaceous
Height: 1.5 metres (5 ft)
Length: 4 metres (13 ft)
Weight: 900 kilograms (1,980 lbs)
How it moved: On all fours
Diet: Herbivorous
Food: Tough vegetation
Main predator: *Daspletosaurus*
Special features: *Avaceratops* had a large cutting area on its beak

Avaceratops's *powerful limbs were embedded in blunt hooves.*

4 metres (13 ft) long

157

Baryonyx

[*Baryonyx* means: Heavy Claw]

? How do you say it?
Bah-ree-on-icks

Baryonyx was a slightly smaller relative of *Spinosaurus* that lived in Europe and Africa about 120 million years ago. Like its larger relative, *Baryonyx* was a bipedal dinosaur that probably specialized in hunting fish – fish scales and bones were found in the stomach cavity of one fossil. It is likely to have snatched at fish in the water using it long jaws or perhaps hooked them out of rivers using its super-long claws.

Dino Fact File

Did you know?

Baryonyx had incredibly long claws on its thumbs – perfect for spearing fish in rivers.

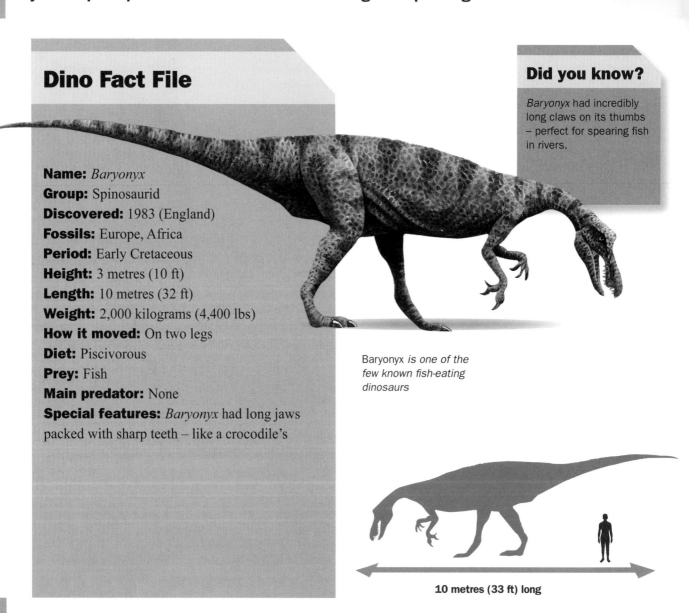

Name: *Baryonyx*
Group: Spinosaurid
Discovered: 1983 (England)
Fossils: Europe, Africa
Period: Early Cretaceous
Height: 3 metres (10 ft)
Length: 10 metres (32 ft)
Weight: 2,000 kilograms (4,400 lbs)
How it moved: On two legs
Diet: Piscivorous
Prey: Fish
Main predator: None
Special features: *Baryonyx* had long jaws packed with sharp teeth – like a crocodile's

Baryonyx *is one of the few known fish-eating dinosaurs*

10 metres (33 ft) long

Brachiosaurus

[*Brachiosaurus* means: **Arm Lizard**]

? How do you say it?
Brak-ee-oh-saw-rus

Brachiosaurus was a long-necked plant-eating sauropod. There were many types of big sauropod in the Late Jurassic period. Some were adapted for grazing on plants that grew close to the ground. Others, like **Brachiosaurus**, were tall so they could eat leaves and needles from high in the trees.

24 metres (79 ft) long

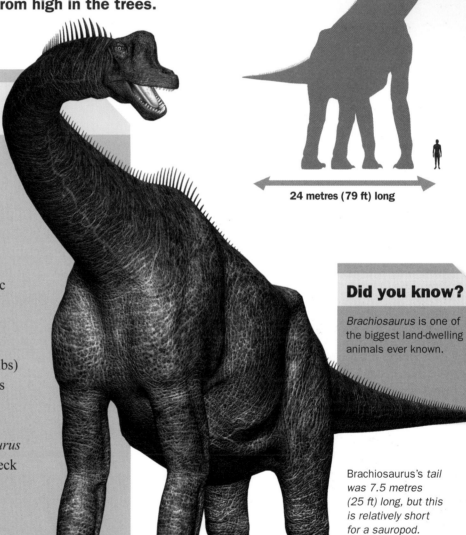

Dino Fact File

Name: *Brachiosaurus*
Group: Sauropod
Discovered: 1909 (Tanzania, Africa)
Fossils: East Africa; Midwestern USA
Period: Mid-to-Late Jurassic
Height: 12 metres (40 ft)
Length: 24 metres (79 ft)
Weight: 33,000–88,000 kilograms (72,750–194,000 lbs)
How it moved: On all fours
Diet: Herbivorous
Food: Leaves, cones
Main predator: *Albertosaurus*
Special features: Long neck and small head

Did you know?

Brachiosaurus is one of the biggest land-dwelling animals ever known.

Brachiosaurus's *tail was 7.5 metres (25 ft) long, but this is relatively short for a sauropod.*

Cornered

1 The young predator *Megalosaurus* and an adult *Camptosaurus* are evenly matched in body mass.

2
They circle one another, each trying to gain an advantage. Suddenly the predator makes its move. It opens its hugh jaws, and starts to back the prey towards a wall of boulders.

Camptosaurus

3
Cornered, **Camptosaurus** turns to face its enemy. Will the young **Megalosaurus's** lack of hunting experience provide the lucky break its victim needs, or will this encounter be fatal?

Turn to page 248 to find out.

Camptosaurus

[*Camptosaurus* means: **Flexible Lizard**]

? **How do you say it?**
Camp-to-saw-rus

Camptosaurus is a Jurassic dinosaur whose fossil remains have been found in both North America and Europe. This herbivore gets its name from its long supple backbone. Its three-toed feet give the name to the ornithopod 'bird-feet' dinosaurs, a group in the ornithischian order. The tightly packed teeth in its cheek, combined with its beak, were perfect for cutting and processing the tough Jurassic vegetation.

Dino Fact File

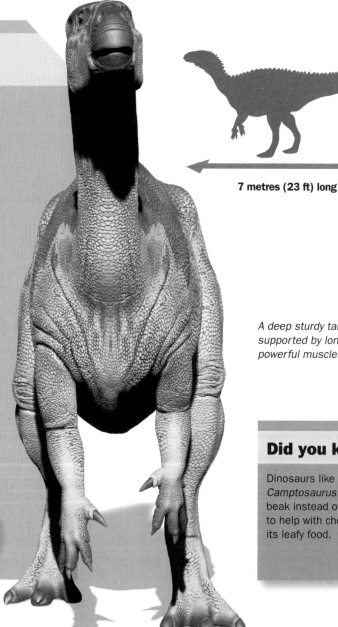

Name: *Camptosaurus*
Group: Ornithopod
Discovered: 1879 (Wyoming, USA)
Fossils: Western parts of the USA
Period: Late Jurassic
Height: 3 metres (10 ft)
Length: 7 metres (23 ft)
Weight: 1,800 kilograms (4,000 lbs)
How it moved: On two legs and on all fours
Diet: Herbivorous
Food: Tough vegetation
Main predator: *Megalosaurus*
Special features: *Camptosaurus* had a small head, a strong beak and lots of grinding teeth

7 metres (23 ft) long

A deep sturdy tail supported by long, powerful muscles.

Turn to page 160 to see how *Camptosaurus* fares in battle against *Megalosaurus*.

Did you know?

Dinosaurs like *Camptosaurus* has a beak instead of soft lips, to help with chopping up its leafy food.

Carcharodontosaurus

[*Carcharodontosaurus* means: **Jagged Tooth Lizard**]

Carcharodontosaurus lived in what is now North Africa, in the mid-Cretaceous period. It was among the biggest and heaviest of the dinosaurs and experts think it also had excellent eyesight. True to its name, this theropod had teeth edged with tiny razor-sharp structures called denticles, perfect for tearing into live flesh.

How do you say it?
Car-ca-roe-don-toe-saw-rus

Dino Fact File

Turn to page 200 to see how *Carcharodontosaurus* fares in battle against *Kaprosuchus*.

Name: *Carcharodontosaurus*
Group: Carcharadontosaurid
Discovered: 1927 (Algeria, North Africa)
Fossils: North Africa
Period: Mid-Cretaceous
Height: 3.9 metres (13 ft)
Length: 11 metres (36 ft)
Weight: 7,000 kilograms (15,400 lbs)
How it moved: On two legs
Diet: Carnivorous
Prey: *Kaprosuchus*
Main predator: None
Special features: This dinosaur had enormous, powerful jaws and sharp teeth that could easily penetrate the toughest skin

11 metres (36 ft) long

A heavy tail with powerful muscles aided locomotion.

Did you know?

Carcharodontosaurus had long and muscular legs and could persure prey at up to 20 mph (32 km/h).

163

Ceratosaurus

[*Ceratosaurus*: **Horned Lizard**]

Ceratosaurus was a large predator that roamed the planet at around the same time as *Allosaurus*, 153–148 million years ago. Large specimens of this dinosaur have been found in Utah and Colorado in the United States, and in Portugal, Europe. *Ceratosaurus* had the most varied diet of all dinosaurs, eating everything from fish to crocodiles to antelope.

Dino Fact File

Name: *Ceratosaurus*
Group: Theropod
Discovered: 1884 (Utah, USA)
Fossils: North America; western Europe
Period: Late Jurassic
Height: 4 metres (13 ft)
Length: 6.7 metres (22 ft)
Weight: 980 kilograms (2,160 lbs)
How it moved: On two legs
Diet: Piscivorous; carnivorous
Prey: Fish, crocodiles, antelope
Main predator: None
Special features: *Ceratosaurus* had a little horn at the end of its snout, and two more horns above the eyes

Did you know?

Some scientists think the horn on the nose might have been used for some kind of butting contest against other male *Ceratosauruses*.

6.7 metres (22 ft) long

Ceratosaurus *had large jaws with blade like teeth.*

Coelophysis

[*Coelophysis* means: **Hollow Form**]

How do you say it?
See-loe-fie-sis

Scientists think that **Coelophysis** lived in herds or in family groups. They think this because they found a large group of **Coelophysis** fossils in one place. This showed that the animals had lived and died together. **Coelophysis** hunted for lizards and smaller dinosaurs, possibly in packs.

Dino Fact File

Name: *Coelophysis*
Group: Coelophysid
Discovered:
1881 (New Mexico, USA)
Fossils: North America
Period: Late Triassic
Height: 1 metre (3 ft)
Length: 3 metres (10 ft)
Weight: 15–20 kilograms (33–44 lbs)
How it moved: On two legs
Diet: Carnivorous
Prey: Small reptiles
Main predator: *Postosuchus*
Special features: *Coelophysis* was a very speedy and agile runner

Coelophysis *had long legs and was a very fast runner.*

Did you know?

Coelphysis's name 'hollow form' derives from the fact that it had hollow vertebrae.

3 metres (10 ft) long

165

Archaeopteryx

1 The late **Jurassic period** has given rise to a wide variety of dinosaurs. Some have even evolved into flying, bird-like animals.

2 Here, an **Archaeopteryx** 'the first bird', leaps into the air, kicking its sharp talons at **Compsognathus.** Its enemy is its closest relative – like two sides of the same coin.

Clashing Cousins

Compsognathus

3 The *Archaeopteryx* was just looking for a break from searching for fish and stumbled into wrong territory – now it faces a standoff with the fierce *Compsognathus.* Who will back down? Who is the superior fighter, the 'first bird' or its land-living cousin?

Turn to page 248 to find out.

Compsognathus

How do you say it?

Comp-sog-nay-thass

[*Compsognathus* means: **Pretty Jaw**]

Compsognathus was one of the smallest dinosaurs. Its body was the size of a chicken. *Compsognathus* was tiny, but it was a fierce hunter. Its long legs show that *Compsognathus* was a fast runner. This dinosaur's long tail helped it to balance when it was running. *Compsognathus* ate lizards. We know this because scientists have found lizard fossils in the stomach of a *Compsognathus* fossil. Scientists think it ate insects, too.

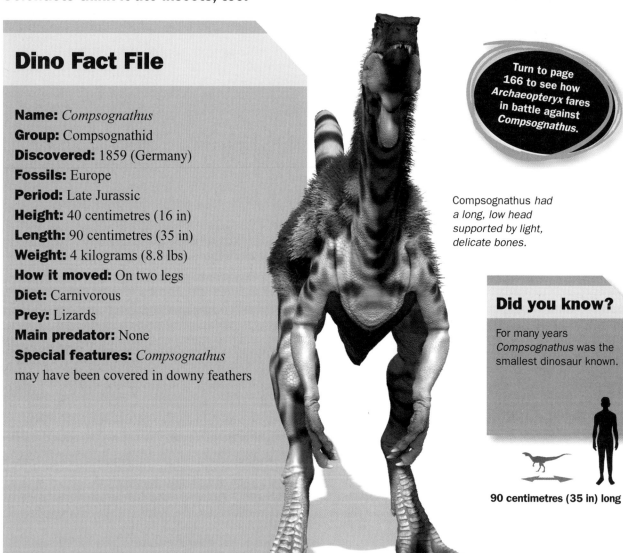

Dino Fact File

Name: *Compsognathus*

Group: Compsognathid

Discovered: 1859 (Germany)

Fossils: Europe

Period: Late Jurassic

Height: 40 centimetres (16 in)

Length: 90 centimetres (35 in)

Weight: 4 kilograms (8.8 lbs)

How it moved: On two legs

Diet: Carnivorous

Prey: Lizards

Main predator: None

Special features: *Compsognathus* may have been covered in downy feathers

Turn to page 166 to see how *Archaeopteryx* fares in battle against *Compsognathus*.

Compsognathus *had a long, low head supported by light, delicate bones.*

Did you know?

For many years *Compsognathus* was the smallest dinosaur known.

90 centimetres (35 in) long

Cryptoclidus

[*Cryptoclidus* means: **Hidden Collarbone**]

? How do you say it?

Crip-toe-clide-us

When **Cryptoclidus** fossils were first discovered, one scientist said that **Cryptoclidus** must have looked like a snake threaded through a turtle. **Cryptoclidus** was a type of plesiosaur. There were short-necked plesiosaurs and long-necked plesiosaurs. **Cryptoclidus** was a long-necked plesiosaur. **Cryptoclidus** flew through the water using paddles.

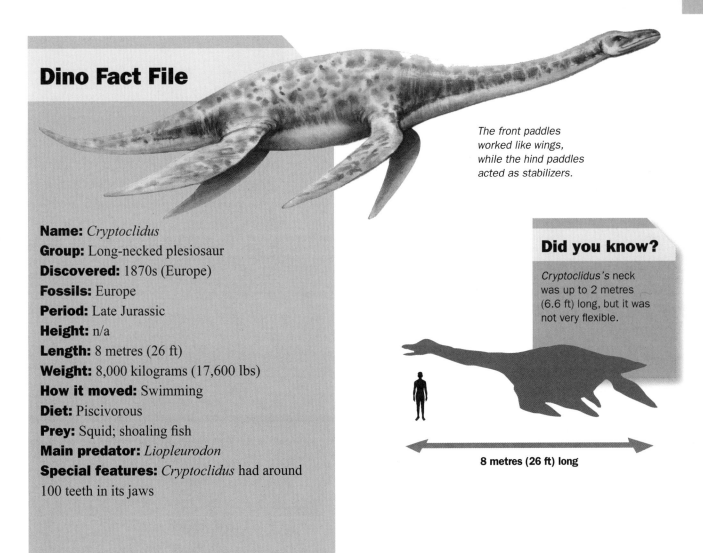

Dino Fact File

The front paddles worked like wings, while the hind paddles acted as stabilizers.

Name: *Cryptoclidus*
Group: Long-necked plesiosaur
Discovered: 1870s (Europe)
Fossils: Europe
Period: Late Jurassic
Height: n/a
Length: 8 metres (26 ft)
Weight: 8,000 kilograms (17,600 lbs)
How it moved: Swimming
Diet: Piscivorous
Prey: Squid; shoaling fish
Main predator: *Liopleurodon*
Special features: *Cryptoclidus* had around 100 teeth in its jaws

Did you know?

Cryptoclidus's neck was up to 2 metres (6.6 ft) long, but it was not very flexible.

8 metres (26 ft) long

Deinonychus

[*Deinonychus* means: **Terrible Claw**]

How do you say it?
Di-non-y-cus

Deinonychus was a fierce dinosaur with very big claws. It could run very fast after its prey. Scientists think that *Deinonychus* hunted in packs. They would gather around their prey and would slash it with their sharp claws. *Deinonychus* had a big brain, so scientists think it was quite clever. *Deinonychus* was the supreme dinosaur predator of its time and for its habitat. It lived in North America during the early part of the Cretaceous period.

Dino Fact File

Turn to page 232 to see how *Tenontosaurus* fares in battle against *Deinonychus*.

Name: *Deinonychus*
Group: Dromaeosaurid
Discovered: 1931 (Montana, USA)
Fossils: North America
Period: Early Cretaceous
Height: 1.25 metres (4.75 ft)
Length: 4 metres (13 ft)
Weight: 75 kilograms (165 lbs)
How it moved: On two legs
Diet: Carnivorous
Prey: *Tenontosaurus*
Main predator: None
Special features: *Deinonychus* had a large brain for its body size

Did you know?

Deinonychus is very similar to *Velociraptor*, but lived many million years earlier.

4 metres (13 ft)

Sickle-shaped claws used to hook into a victim's flesh.

Dilophosaurus

[*Dilophosaurus* means: **Double-crested Lizard**]

? How do you say it?

Die-lo-pho-saw-rus

Dilophosaurus lived during the early part of the Jurassic period. This carnivore had a distinctive crest made up of two bony ridges along the top of its skull. It is believed that this strip could have been used for communication or for mating displays. The fossil remains of *Dilophosaurus* were discovered in 1942 in Arizona, USA, by the palaeontologist Samuel Welles.

Dino Fact File

Name: *Dilophosaurus*
Group: Theropod
Discovered: 1942 (Arizona, USA)
Fossils: North America
Period: Early Jurassic
Height: 2 metres (6.5 ft)
Length: 7 metres (23 ft)
Weight: 350 kilograms (772 lbs)
How it moved: On two legs
Diet: Carnivorous
Prey: Small animals
Main predator: None
Special features: It had strange crests on its head, possibly for attracting a mate

Did you know?

Some scientists think that *Dilophosaurus* migh have fed only on carrion – that is, the carcasses of dead animals.

7 metres (23 ft) long

Dilophosaurus *had an unusually long tail for an active predator.*

Turn to page 172 to see how Anchisaurus fares in battle against Dilophosaurus.

Fresh Meat

Dilophosaurus

1 The **Jurassic period** has begun. The dinosaurs are getting bigger and becoming more dominant.

2 Plant-eating dinosaurs, such as **Anchisaurus**, have now evolved. These docile animals are only about the weight of a small human and can become prey for their bigger carnivorous cousins.

Anchisaurus

3 One such carnivore, **Dilophosaurus,** gives chase to a family of **Anchisauruses**. The herbivores scuttle away, seeking refuge in the safety of their herd. Will **Dilophosaurus** manage to pick one of them off?

Turn to page 248 to find out.

Dimorphodon

[*Dimorphodon* means: **Two-form Tooth**]

? **How do you say it?** *Die-mor-foh-don*

Dimorphodon was a pterosaur with a big beak. Scientists think the beak might have been colourful like that of a modern-day toucan. *Dimorphodons* might have used their beaks for signalling to each other. Scientists have used fossil footprints to work out how *Dimorphodons* walked. They have found footprints that show four sets of tracks. This means they walked on their back legs, using their arms like walking sticks.

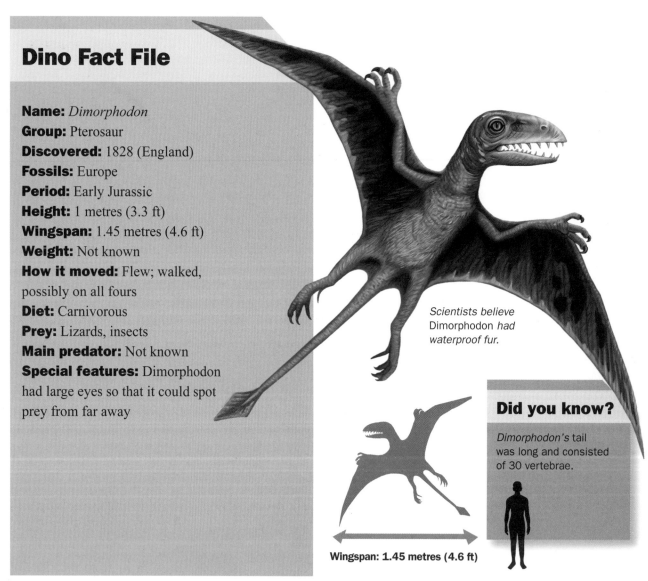

Dino Fact File

Name: *Dimorphodon*
Group: Pterosaur
Discovered: 1828 (England)
Fossils: Europe
Period: Early Jurassic
Height: 1 metres (3.3 ft)
Wingspan: 1.45 metres (4.6 ft)
Weight: Not known
How it moved: Flew; walked, possibly on all fours
Diet: Carnivorous
Prey: Lizards, insects
Main predator: Not known
Special features: Dimorphodon had large eyes so that it could spot prey from far away

Scientists believe Dimorphodon *had waterproof fur.*

Wingspan: 1.45 metres (4.6 ft)

Did you know?

Dimorphodon's tail was long and consisted of 30 vertebrae.

Diplodocus

[*Diplodocus* means: **Double Beamed**]

How do you say it?
Dip-low-doh-cus

The biggest dinosaurs of all were the sauropods. They were herbivores with long necks. *Diplodocus* was a sauropod that walked on all fours. It ate ferns from the ground and sometimes it would rise up on its back legs to eat leaves from trees. *Diplodocus* was so big, it had to keep eating all the time! To help grind up food in its stomach, it swallowed stones.

Dino Fact File

Name: *Diplodocus*
Group: Sauropod
Discovered: 1877 (USA)
Fossils: USA
Period: Late Jurassic
Hip height: 5 metres (16.5 feet)
Length: 27 metres (88.5 ft)
Weight: 15,000 kilograms (33,000 tons)
How it moved: On all fours
Diet: Herbivorous
Prey: Conifers
Main predator: *Allosaurus*
Special features: Spines along neck, back and tail

Did you know?

Diplodocus used its peg-like teeth to strip needles from trees. It swallowed them whole.

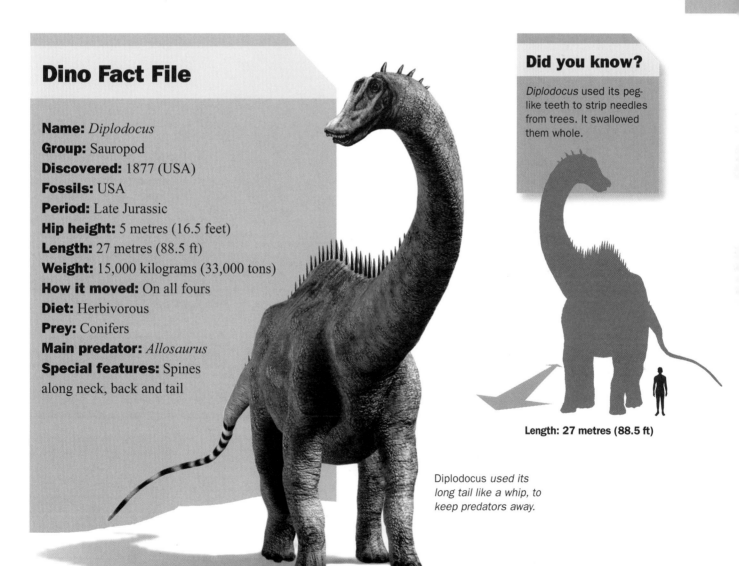

Length: 27 metres (88.5 ft)

Diplodocus used its long tail like a whip, to keep predators away.

175

Dsungaripterus

[*Dsungaripterus* means: **Wing from Junggar in China**]

Dsungaripterus fossils were the first pterosaur fossils to be found in China. Just like some modern-day birds, some flying reptiles had crests on their heads. They used them to signal to each other. *Dsungaripterus* probably ate shellfish – its pointed jaws could dig shellfish out of little holes in rocks. It had tooth-like knobs at the back of its mouth, which would have been able to crush the shells.

How do you say it?

Zung-a-rip-ter-us

Dino Fact File

Name: *Dsungaripterus*
Group: Pterodactyloid
Discovered: 1964 (China)
Fossils: China
Period: Early Cretaceous
Height: Not known
Wingspan: 3 metres (10 ft)
Weight: Not known
How it moved: Flying; walking on two legs or perhaps on all fours
Diet: Piscivorous
Prey: Shellfish
Main predator: Not known
Special features: A bony crest running along its snout

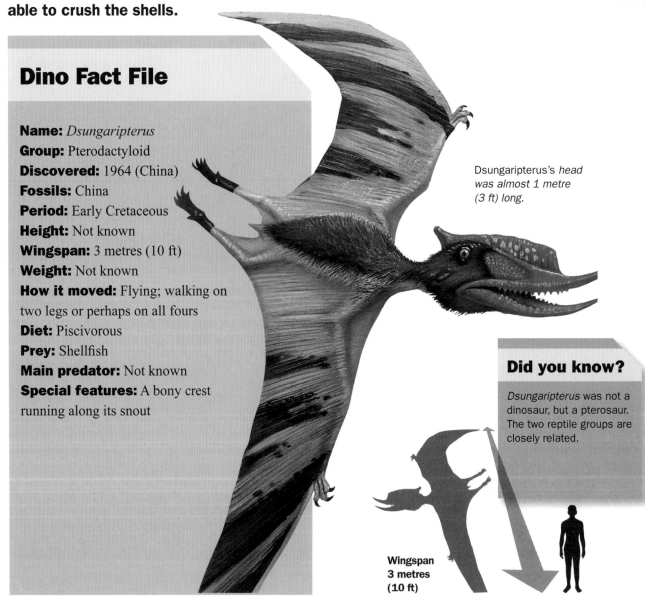

Dsungaripterus's *head was almost 1 metre (3 ft) long.*

Did you know?

Dsungaripterus was not a dinosaur, but a pterosaur. The two reptile groups are closely related.

Wingspan 3 metres (10 ft)

Elasmosaurus

[*Elasmosaurus* means: **Long Lizard**]

? How do you say it?

Ee-laz-moh-saw-rus

Elasmosaurus was a giant swimming reptile with a very long neck. It swam using its paddles in a flying motion. Modern-day sea lions swim like this. As it swam along, *Elasmosaurus* could use its long neck to reach out and grab fish.

Dino Fact File

Name: *Elasmosaurus*
Group: Plesiosaur
Discovered: 1867 (USA)
Fossils: Kansas, USA
Period: Late Cretaceous
Hip height: 2 metres (6.5 ft)
Length: 13 metres (42.5 ft)
Weight: 6,000 kilograms (13,230 lbs)
How it moved: Swimming
Diet: Piscivorous
Prey: Ammonites, fish
Main predator: Pliosaurs
Special features: *Elasmosaurus* had a long neck with 71 vertebrae

Did you know?

Although *Elasmosaurus* lived in the water, it had to come to the surface to breathe.

13 metres (42.5 ft) long

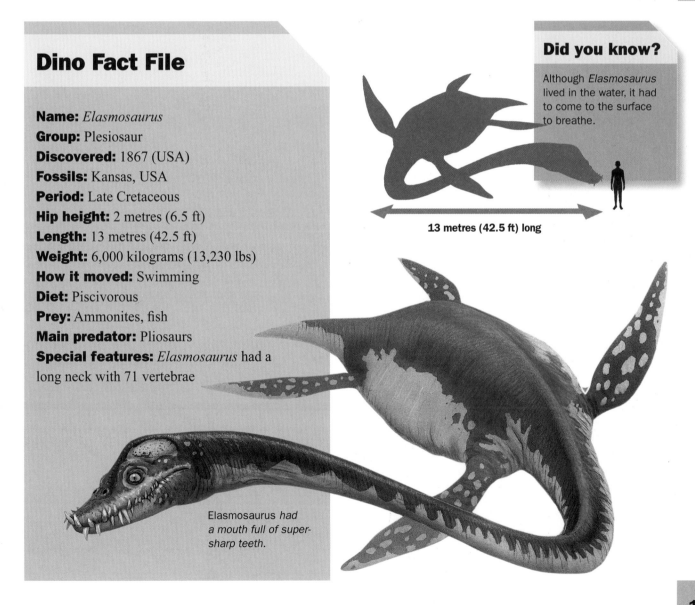

Elasmosaurus *had a mouth full of super-sharp teeth.*

Jaws

1 **We are in the Triassic period.** The first dinosaurs have evolved from their reptilian ancestors. They are agile, fast, clawed and sharp-toothed carnivores.

Herrerasaurus

2

In what is now South America, two dinosaur species, *Herrerasaurus* and *Eoraptor*, compete for food. *Herrerasaurus* is a big beast, weighing about as much as a polar bear, but *Eoraptor* is the faster animal.

3

Herrerasaurus gives chase to three *Eoraptors*, who have dared to enter its cave in search of a possible carcass to steal. One is already wounded, and all three are retreating as fast as they can but the snapping jaws are drawing in.

Turn to page 248 to see what happens.

Eoraptor

Eoraptor

[*Eoraptor* means: **Dawn Thief**]

? **How do you say it?**

E-oh-rap-tor

Eoraptor was one of the first dinosaurs to live on Earth. It was a tiny carnivore about the size of a fox. *Eoraptor* lived millions of years before *Allosaurus* and *T. rex*. However, it had the same body shape as the big meat-eaters who came after it. This fast, fierce little dinosaur hunted for lizards and insects. It had five fingers on each hand for grabbing prey.

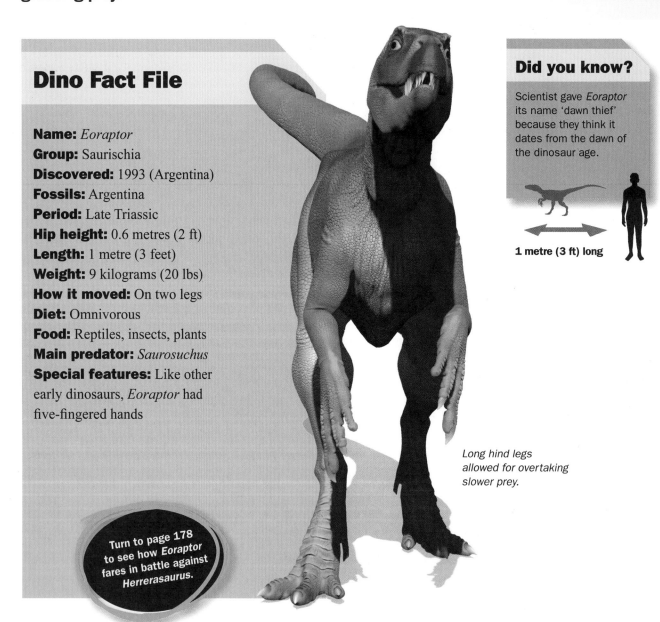

Dino Fact File

Name: *Eoraptor*

Group: Saurischia

Discovered: 1993 (Argentina)

Fossils: Argentina

Period: Late Triassic

Hip height: 0.6 metres (2 ft)

Length: 1 metre (3 feet)

Weight: 9 kilograms (20 lbs)

How it moved: On two legs

Diet: Omnivorous

Food: Reptiles, insects, plants

Main predator: *Saurosuchus*

Special features: Like other early dinosaurs, *Eoraptor* had five-fingered hands

Did you know?

Scientist gave *Eoraptor* its name 'dawn thief' because they think it dates from the dawn of the dinosaur age.

1 metre (3 ft) long

Long hind legs allowed for overtaking slower prey.

Turn to page 178 to see how *Eoraptor* fares in battle against *Herrerasaurus*.

Gastonia

[*Gastonia* is named after **Robert Gaston**]

How do you say it?

Gas-toe-near

Gastonia was an ankylosaur of the Cretaceous period. These herbivorous dinosaurs were built for protection against carnivorous predators. Rows of bony spines running from *Gastonia's* head to its tail provided a living suit of armour. In an attack, *Gastonia's* short limbs meant it could quickly lie down and display its spiky armour. *Gastonia's* tough beak was designed to harvest its food, and its small, leaf-shaped, serrated teeth were adapted to slice up vegetation.

Dino Fact File

Turn to page 248 to see how *Gastonia* fares in battle against *Utahraptor*.

Name: *Gastonia*
Group: Ankylosaur
Discovered: 1989 (Utah, USA)
Fossils: USA
Period: Cretaceous
Height: 1.8 metres (6 ft)
Length: 6 metres (19.5 ft)
Weight: 1,500 kilograms (3,300 lbs)
How it moved: On all fours
Diet: Herbivorous
Food: Plants
Main predator: *Utahraptor*
Special features: *Gastonia* had wide, flat, bony spines covering the neck, back and tail

Did you know?

The longest of *Gastonia's* spines reached lengths of 30 centimetres (12 in).

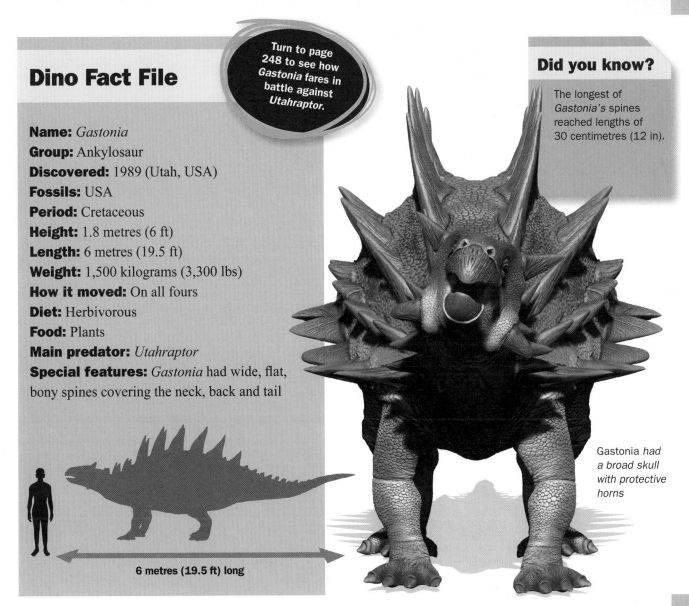

Gastonia *had a broad skull with protective horns*

6 metres (19.5 ft) long

181

1 The huge, sickle-shaped claws of *Utahraptor* have found a grip between the bony spikes of its dumpy *Gastonia* prey. It has not eaten for over a week and will now tackle anything – even this tank of a beast.

Claws
on Armour

Utahraptor

2 The stricken *Gastonia* spins around, trying to unbalance its piggy-back attacker. But *Utahraptor* hangs on, biting again and again into the few unarmoured areas of the ankylosaur's back with its razor-sharp teeth.

3 If it can just keep this up, the battle could soon be over. Can *Utahraptor* really fell a prey such as *Gastonia*?

Turn to page 248 to find out.

Giganotosaurus?

How do you say it?
Ji-gan-oh-toe-saw-rus

[*Giganotosaurus* means: **Giant Southern Lizard**]

Giganotosaurus was probably the biggest meat-eating dinosaur. It was longer than T. rex, but it was not as heavy. It had jaws that could swallow you whole! Some of its teeth were 15 centimetres (6 in) long! Scientists have not yet found many fossils of *Giganotosaurus*, so they are not quite sure what it really looked like.

Dino Fact File

Name: *Giganotosaurus*
Group: Carcharodontosaurid
Discovered: 1993 (Argentina)
Fossils: Argentina
Period: Late Cretaceous
Hip height: 4.6 metres (15 ft)
Length: 12 metres (40 ft)
Weight: 8,000 kilograms (18,000 lbs)
How it moved: On all fours
Diet: Carnivorous
Prey: *Argentinosaurus*
Main predator: None
Special features: The jaws were rammed with teeth that had serrated edges for slicing through flesh.

Giganotosaurus *hunted by charging at its prey with its jaws wide open.*

12 metres (40 ft) long

Did you know?

Giganotosaurus skulls could reach 1.95 metres (6 ft) in length, but these dinosaurs still had very small brains.

Gorgosaurus

[*Gorgosaurus* means: **Dreadful Lizard**]

How do you say it?
Gore-go-saw-rus

Gorgosaurus was a member of the biggest and fiercest dinosaur group – the tyrannosaurs. Like other tyrannosaurs, *Gorgosaurus* was a top predator, a massive beast with huge legs, short arms and immensely powerful jaws. *Gorgosaurus* would have preyed on the many plant-eating dinosaurs that shared its environment, perhaps picking off weak members of the herd.

Dino Fact File

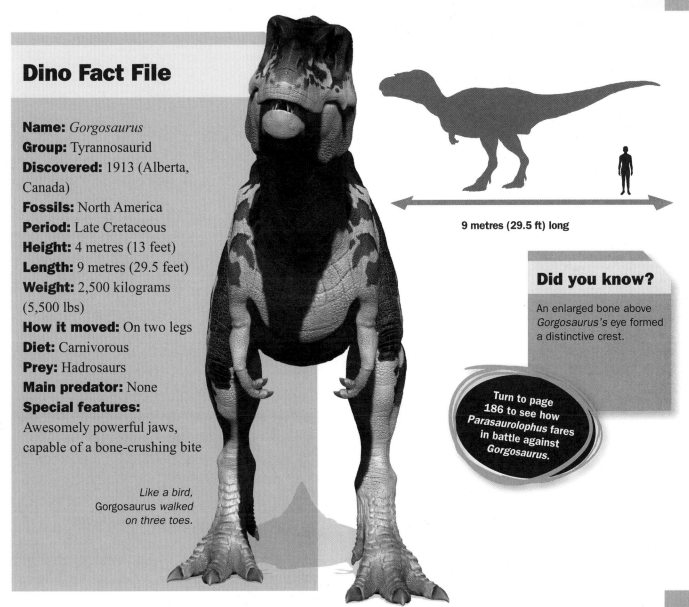

Name: *Gorgosaurus*
Group: Tyrannosaurid
Discovered: 1913 (Alberta, Canada)
Fossils: North America
Period: Late Cretaceous
Height: 4 metres (13 feet)
Length: 9 metres (29.5 feet)
Weight: 2,500 kilograms (5,500 lbs)
How it moved: On two legs
Diet: Carnivorous
Prey: Hadrosaurs
Main predator: None
Special features: Awesomely powerful jaws, capable of a bone-crushing bite

Like a bird, Gorgosaurus walked on three toes.

9 metres (29.5 ft) long

Did you know?

An enlarged bone above *Gorgosaurus*'s eye formed a distinctive crest.

Turn to page 186 to see how *Parasaurolophus* fares in battle against *Gorgosaurus*.

1 One of the *Parasaurolophus* herd has been injured and the other members can hear it bellowing in pain. Like all *hadrosaurs*, the *Parasaurolophus* can make deep, booming sounds through its head crest.

Gorgosaurus

The Last Lunge

Parasaurolophus

2 The herd rushes towards the stricken sound, but an adult **Gorgosaurus** has responded to the call too. The **Gorgosaurus** stumbles clumsily into their path, its right leg dragging on the ground. It seems to be injured.

3 Nevertheless the **Gorgosaurus** lunges at the closest **Parasaurolophus**. It is aiming for a crushing bite that will break the animal's spine, but its jaws are too weak to make contact with the bone. Can the *hadrosaurs* shake off this annoying predator and continue their rescue operation?

Turn to page 248 to find out.

Guanlong

[*Guanlong* means: **Crowned Dragon**]

? How do you say it?

Gwan-long

The most famous meat-eating dinosaur ever must be *Tyrannosaurus rex*. *Guanlong* was one of its earliest relatives, although it was small in comparison, and had a similar head shape. It was just as fierce, however, even though it hunted smaller prey. Scientists think the small meat-eating dinosaurs were warm-blooded and probably had feathery coverings.

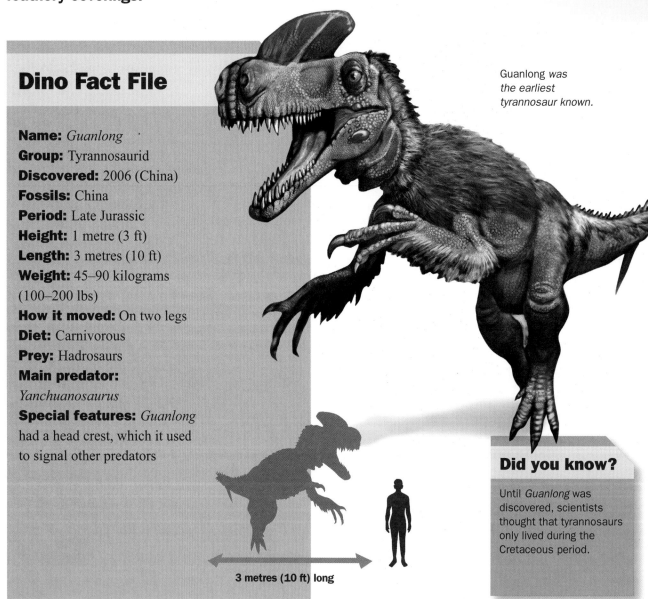

Guanlong was the earliest tyrannosaur known.

Dino Fact File

Name: *Guanlong*
Group: Tyrannosaurid
Discovered: 2006 (China)
Fossils: China
Period: Late Jurassic
Height: 1 metre (3 ft)
Length: 3 metres (10 ft)
Weight: 45–90 kilograms (100–200 lbs)
How it moved: On two legs
Diet: Carnivorous
Prey: Hadrosaurs
Main predator: *Yanchuanosaurus*
Special features: *Guanlong* had a head crest, which it used to signal other predators

3 metres (10 ft) long

Did you know?

Until *Guanlong* was discovered, scientists thought that tyrannosaurs only lived during the Cretaceous period.

Hadrosaurus

[*Hadrosaurus* means: **Sturdy Lizard]**

? How do you say it?
Had-ro-saw-rus

Hadrosaurus was one of the 'duck-billed' dinosaurs. We call them that because they had mouths that looked a bit like ducks' beaks. The beak was used for scraping the needles from conifer trees. *Hadrosaurus* had lots of grinding teeth in its mouth. It used them for crunching up tough plants. Its long tail helped it to balance when it walked on two legs.

Dino Fact File

Name: *Hadrosaurus*
Group: Ornithopod
Discovered: 1858 (New Jersey, USA)
Fossils: USA
Period: Late Cretaceous
Height: 3 metres (10 ft)
Length: 7 metres (23 ft)
Weight: 7,000 kilograms (15,400 lbs)
How it moved: On all four; raised on two legs to eat
Diet: Herbivorous
Food: Conifers
Main predator: Not known
Special features: Numerous teeth in its jaws, used for grinding its food

Did you know?

Hadrosaurus was the first almost complete dinosaur to be discovered in the United States.

7 metres (23 ft) long

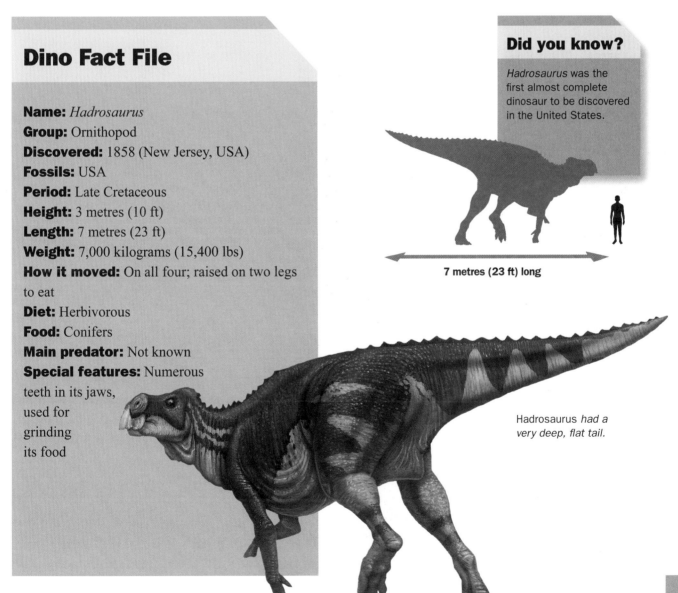

Hadrosaurus *had a very deep, flat tail.*

Herrerasaurus

[*Herrerasaurus* means: **Herrera's Lizard**]

How do you say it?

Huh-rer-ra-saw-rus

Herrerasaurus is named after the Argentinian rancher who found the first fossil specimen. When a complete skeleton was discovered, it showed that **Herrerasaurus** was a predatory dinosaur. Amazingly, humans are much closer in time to **Tyrannosaurus rex** than **Herrerasaurus** was, but experts believe that this early predator was in fact **T. rex's** distant ancestor.

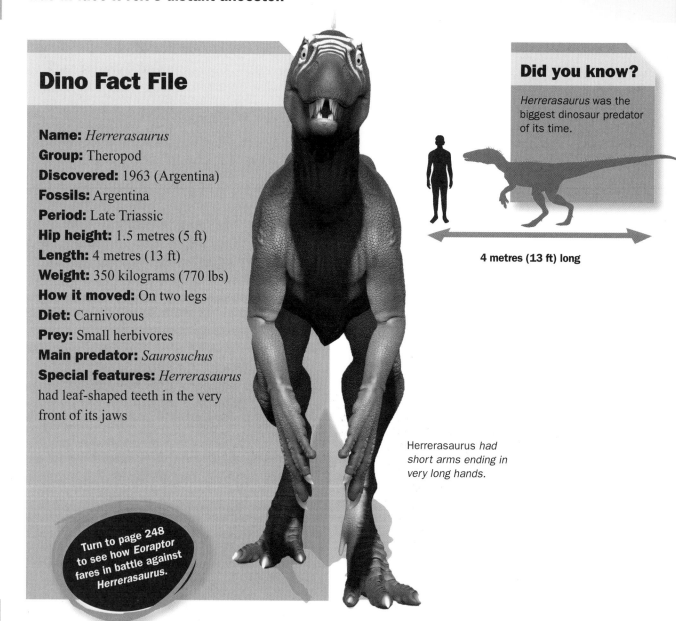

Dino Fact File

Name: *Herrerasaurus*
Group: Theropod
Discovered: 1963 (Argentina)
Fossils: Argentina
Period: Late Triassic
Hip height: 1.5 metres (5 ft)
Length: 4 metres (13 ft)
Weight: 350 kilograms (770 lbs)
How it moved: On two legs
Diet: Carnivorous
Prey: Small herbivores
Main predator: *Saurosuchus*
Special features: *Herrerasaurus* had leaf-shaped teeth in the very front of its jaws

Did you know?

Herrerasaurus was the biggest dinosaur predator of its time.

4 metres (13 ft) long

Herrerasaurus *had short arms ending in very long hands.*

Turn to page 248 to see how *Eoraptor* fares in battle against *Herrerasaurus*.

Heterodontosaurus

[*Heterodontosaurus* means: **Lizard with Differently Shaped Teeth**]

Heterodontosaurus looked like a fierce carnivore, but it was actually a small herbivore. It had nipping teeth inside its beak and tusks at the side. At the back of its jaws it had grinding teeth for crunching up plants. *Heterodontosaurus* probably looked fierce to scare away predators. If scaring a predator didn't work, it could run away fast on its long legs.

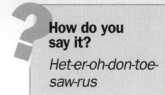

How do you say it?

Het-er-oh-don-toe-saw-rus

Dino Fact File

Name: *Heterodontosaurus*
Group: Ornithopod
Discovered: 1966 (South Africa)
Fossils: South Africa
Period: Early Jurassic
Length: 1.2 metres (4 ft)
Weight: 20 kilograms (44 lbs)
How it moved: On two legs
Diet: Herbivorous
Prey: tough plants, roots
Main predator: *Syntarsus*
Special features: Three kinds of teeth: nipping teeth in the beak; tusks on the sidel; grinding teeth at the back

Did you know?

Heterodontosaurus probably scared away enemies by pretending to look fearsome.

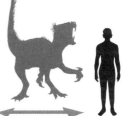

1.2 metres (4 ft) long

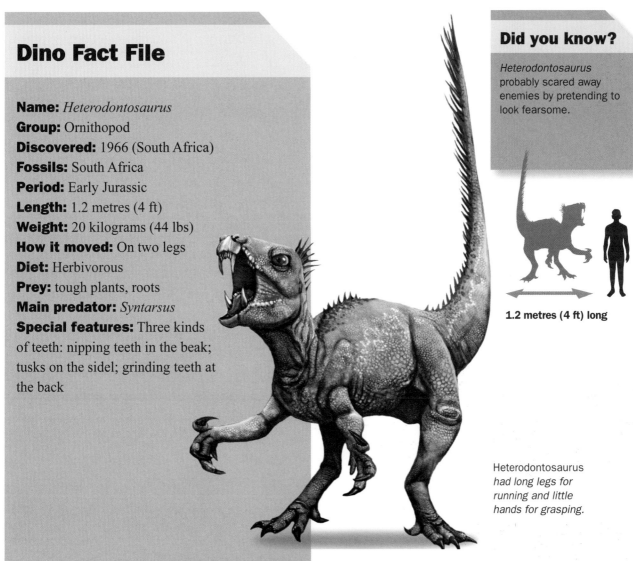

Heterodontosaurus had long legs for running and little hands for grasping.

1 The day is warm and the sun high in the sky. A group of **Albertosauruses** is dozing in the cool shade of some monkey puzzle trees when a family of **Hypacrosauruses** ambles into their view.

A Chance Ambush

2 The herbivores graze in the clearing, unaware of the predators. Suddenly alert, the **Albertosauruses** rise stealthily to their feet. Two prowl around the fearful **Hypacrosaurus** family.

Albertosaurus

3 The roar of these two attackers distracts the prey from the silent, large male beast on their right side. It is selecting which animal to isolate for an attack.

Hypacrosaurus

4

The young *Hypacrosaurus* makes a desperate lunge away from its assailant – only to find itself head-to-head with another pack member. Instantly, the powerful jaws of *Albertosaurus* clamp down hard on the base of the prey's neck.

5 The sound of bones breaking brings a triumphant roar from the hungry pack. Dinner is served.

Hypacrosaurus ?

How do you say it?
Hi-pack-row-saw-rus

[*Hypacrosaurus* means: **Near the Highest Lizard**]

Hypacrosaurus was one of the biggest dinosaurs of its time. Like other lambeosaurs, it was a bipedal and quadrupedal herbivore, and had a head crest and a duckbill. From studying fossilized tracks, experts think that lambeosaurs probably lived in herds. There is also evidence that they may have formed nesting colonies, just as some birds do.

Dino Fact File

Name: *Hypacrosaurus*
Group: Lambeosaur
Discovered: 1910 (Alberta, Canada)
Fossils: Canada, North America
Period: Late Cretaceous
Height: 3.5 metres (11.5 ft)
Length: 10 metres (33 ft)
Weight: 4,000 kilograms (8,800 lbs)
How it moved: On all fours; raised on two legs to eat
Diet: Herbivorous
Food: Plants
Main predator: *Albertosaurus*
Special features: Unlike other dinosaurs of its kind, *Hypacrosaurus* had tall backbones

10 metres (33 ft) long

Relatively delicate forelimbs indicate that most weight was borne by the hind legs.

Turn to pages 192–195 to see how *Hypacrosaurus* fares in battle against *Albertosaurus*.

Did you know?

Scientists used to think that *Hypacrosaurus's* long, strong tail was used for swimming, but experts now know that this dinosaur lived on land.

Ichthyosaurus

[*Ichthyosaurus* means: **Fish Lizard**]

? **How do you say it?**
Ik-thee-oh-saw-rus

Ichthyosaurus was a small swimming reptile. It looked a bit like a shark or a dolphin. It could swim fast and used its speed to chase and catch fish. *Ichthyosaurus* had a tail like a fish, a shark-like fin on its back and paddles for legs. This marine reptile did not lay eggs like many other marine reptiles. Instead, it gave birth to live babies underwater.

Dino Fact File

Name: *Ichthyosaurus*
Group: Ichthyosaur
Discovered: 1811 (England)
Fossils: England, Germany
Period: Late Triassic/Early Jurassic
Height: 50 centimetres (1.75 ft)
Length: 2 metres (6.6 ft)
Weight: 90 kilograms (200 lbs)
How it moved: Swimming
Diet: Piscivorous
Prey: Fish, belemnites
Main predator: Pliosaurs
Special features: It is thought that *Ichthyosaurus* gave birth to live young.

Did you know?

The first complete *Ichthyosaurus* fossil was excavated in Lyme Regis, England, by 12-year-old Mary Anning.

2 metres (6.6 ft) long

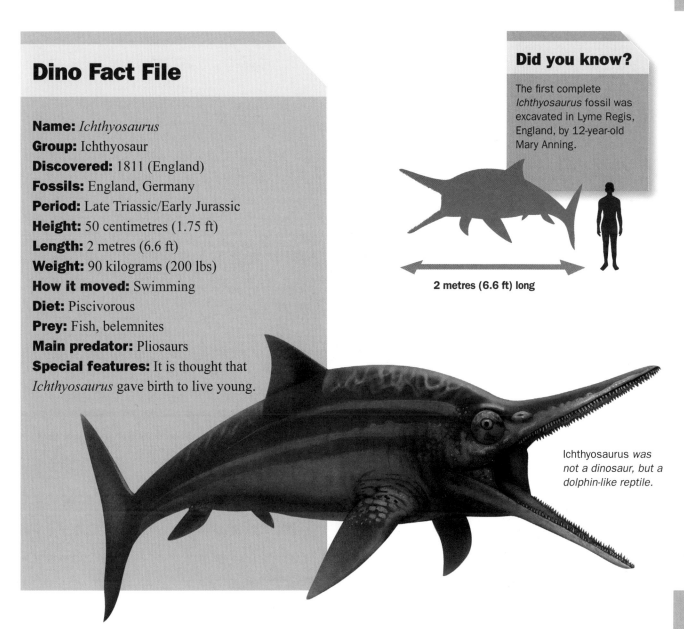

Ichthyosaurus *was not a dinosaur, but a dolphin-like reptile.*

Iguanodon

[*Iguanodon* means: Iguana-toothed]

? How do you say it?
Ig-wah-no-don

Iguanodon was one of the first dinosaurs to be discovered. At first, scientists thought they had found fossils from a fish or a hippopotamus. But then they realised they had found something new – a dinosaur! *Iguanodon* was a bit like a modern-day iguana – only much BIGGER! *Iguanodon* lived in herds. They moved from one area to another to find reeds to eat.

Turn to page 206 to see how Neovenator fares in battle against Iguanodon

Dino Fact File

Name: *Iguanodon*
Group: Ornithopod
Discovered: 1822 (England)
Fossils: Europe, Mongolia, USA
Period: Early Cretaceous
Hip height: 3.8 metres (12.5 ft)
Length: 10 metres (33 ft)
Weight: 5,000 kilograms (11,000 lbs)
How it moved: On all fours, but raised on two to eat foliage from trees
Diet: Herbivorous
Food: Conifers, cycad plants
Main predator:
Megalosaurus
Special features:
Specialized hands with thumb-spike, three hooved fingers and thin, flexible fifth finger

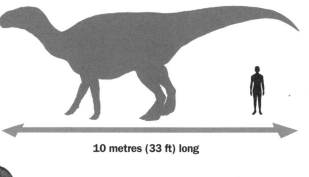

10 metres (33 ft) long

Iguanodon had a long, low skull, not dissimilar to modern horses.

Did you know?

Fossilized footprints show that *Iguanodon* moved around as part of a herd.

Kaprosuchus

[*Kaprosuchus* means: **Boar Crocodile**]

? **How do you say it?** *Cap-pro-sue-cus*

Kaprosuchus was a large crocodylomorph – a vast, semi-aquatic predator similar to a crocodile. Its name, boar crocodile, comes from its huge, pig-like, overlapping teeth. Just like today's crocodiles, *Kaprosuchus* would lie just beneath the water's surface at the edge of a river or lake, waiting for an unsuspecting victim to pass by. Then it would burst up, seize the terrified creature in its massive teeth and drag the prey to a watery grave – the perfect ambush!

Dino Fact File

Name: *Kaprosuchus*
Group: Crocodylomorph
Discovered: 2009 (Niger, West Africa)
Fossils: Niger, West Africa
Period: Late Cretaceous
Height: 1.5 metres (5 ft)
Length: 5 metres (16.5 ft)
Weight: 900 kilograms (1,985 lbs)
How it moved: On all fours
Diet: Carnivorous
Prey: Land animals
Main predator:
Carcharadontosaurus
Special features: Small bony plates beneath the skin's surface provided excellent armour

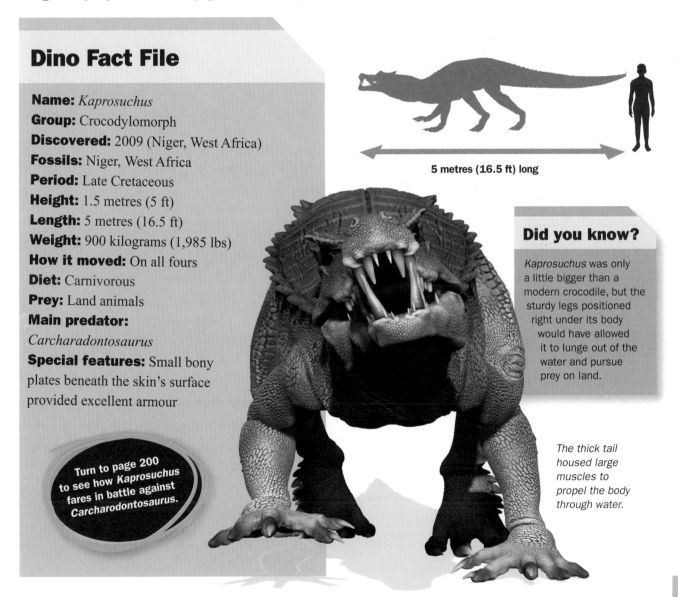

5 metres (16.5 ft) long

Turn to page 200 to see how *Kaprosuchus* fares in battle against *Carcharodontosaurus*.

Did you know?

Kaprosuchus was only a little bigger than a modern crocodile, but the sturdy legs positioned right under its body would have allowed it to lunge out of the water and pursue prey on land.

The thick tail housed large muscles to propel the body through water.

Crocodile Jaws

1 Spying a dozing *Carcharodontosaurus* on the shore, croc *Kaprosuchus* slithers out of the lake and approaches the sleeping predator. Here is an opportunity it can't pass up. Using its stereoscopic vision, the croc lunges at the throat of the dozing giant.

Carcharodontosaurus

2

Carcharodontosaurus leaps awake, roaring with pain and alarm as dagger-like teeth tear into its flesh. It will need to fight hard for its life. Will the unforgiving jaws of croc **Kaprosuchus** end the reign of this mighty predator?

Turn to page 249 to find out.

Kaprosuchus

Kronosaurus

[*Kronosaurus* means: **Kronos Lizard**]

? **How do you say it?**
Kro-no-saw-rus

Kronosaurus had a short neck and a head that was nearly 3 metres (10 ft) long! It probably fed on shellfish, octopus and giant squid. It gets its name from Cronos, a giant in stories from ancient Greece. *Kronosaurus* looked a bit like a modern-day whale. It swam like a modern-day turtle, paddling with its four flippers.

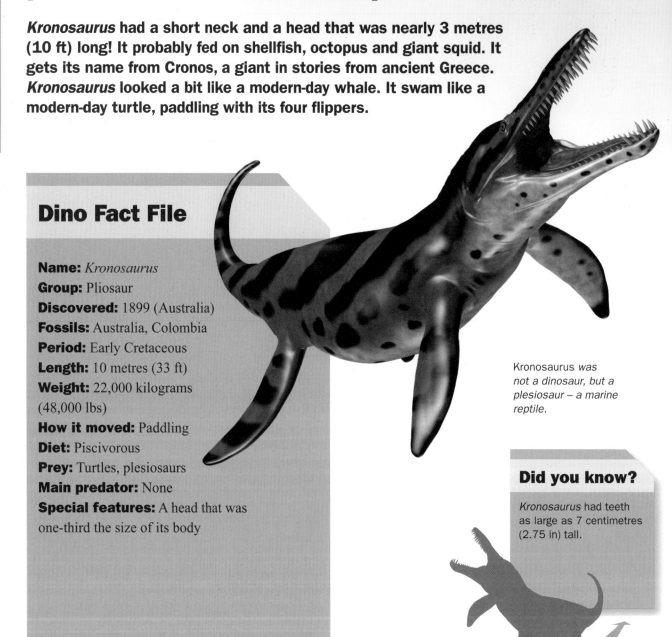

Dino Fact File

Name: *Kronosaurus*
Group: Pliosaur
Discovered: 1899 (Australia)
Fossils: Australia, Colombia
Period: Early Cretaceous
Length: 10 metres (33 ft)
Weight: 22,000 kilograms (48,000 lbs)
How it moved: Paddling
Diet: Piscivorous
Prey: Turtles, plesiosaurs
Main predator: None
Special features: A head that was one-third the size of its body

Kronosaurus was not a dinosaur, but a plesiosaur – a marine reptile.

Did you know?

Kronosaurus had teeth as large as 7 centimetres (2.75 in) tall.

10 metres (33 ft) long

Liopleurodon

[*Liopleurodon* means: **Smooth-sided Tooth**]

Liopleurodon was one of the biggest hunters ever to live on Earth. It was a HUGE, short-necked plesiosaur. *Liopleurodon* had teeth that were 20 centimetres (8 in) long! Scientists have found bite marks from *Liopleurodon* on fossils of large ichthyosaurs and plesiosaurs. *Liopleurodon* would swallow stones to help it sink in the water. If it wanted to rise up to chase prey, it would spit the stones out.

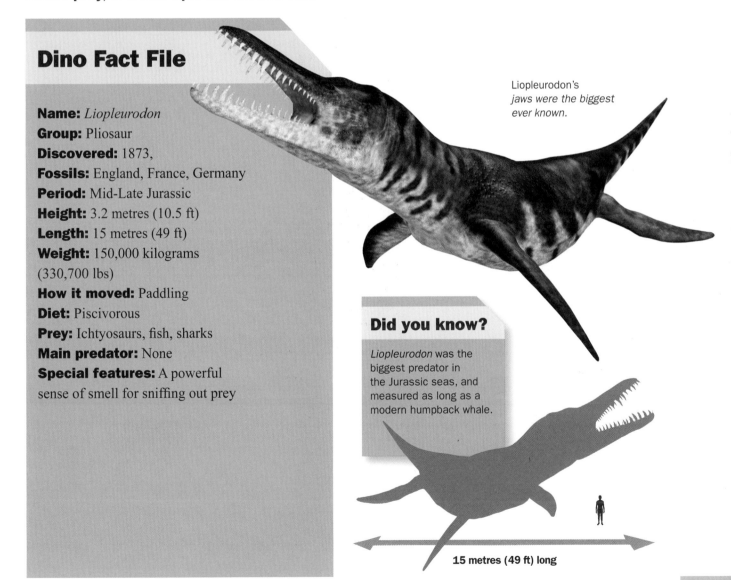

Dino Fact File

Name: *Liopleurodon*
Group: Pliosaur
Discovered: 1873,
Fossils: England, France, Germany
Period: Mid-Late Jurassic
Height: 3.2 metres (10.5 ft)
Length: 15 metres (49 ft)
Weight: 150,000 kilograms (330,700 lbs)
How it moved: Paddling
Diet: Piscivorous
Prey: Ichtyosaurs, fish, sharks
Main predator: None
Special features: A powerful sense of smell for sniffing out prey

Liopleurodon's jaws were the biggest ever known.

Did you know?

Liopleurodon was the biggest predator in the Jurassic seas, and measured as long as a modern humpback whale.

15 metres (49 ft) long

203

Megalosaurus

[*Megalosaurus* means: **Great Lizard**]

? **How do you say it?** *Mef-a-low-saw-rus*

In 1824, British scientist William Buckland named the fossilized bones of a giant, lizard-type animal. He called it *Megalosaurus*, which means great lizard. It would be another 20 years before the word dinosaur was coined. No complete skeleton has been discovered yet, so scientists can't say exactly how *Megalosaurus* looked, but they do know that it was carnivorous and belonged to the theropod group.

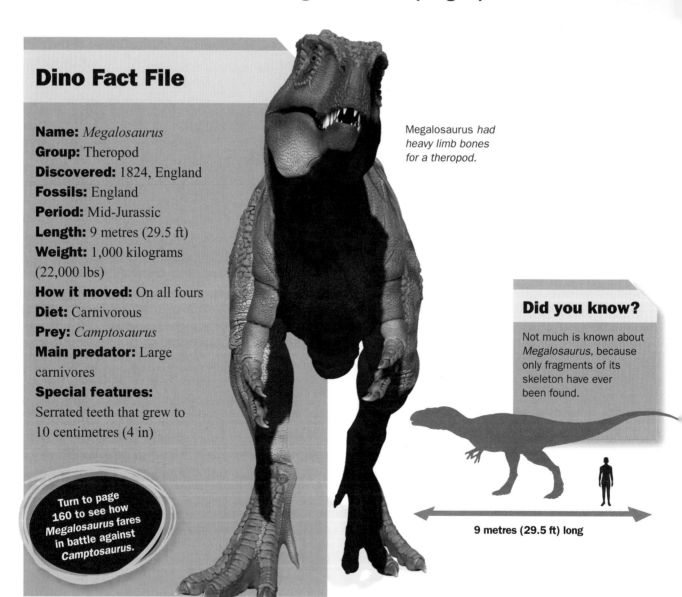

Dino Fact File

Name: *Megalosaurus*

Group: Theropod

Discovered: 1824, England

Fossils: England

Period: Mid-Jurassic

Length: 9 metres (29.5 ft)

Weight: 1,000 kilograms (22,000 lbs)

How it moved: On all fours

Diet: Carnivorous

Prey: *Camptosaurus*

Main predator: Large carnivores

Special features: Serrated teeth that grew to 10 centimetres (4 in)

Megalosaurus *had heavy limb bones for a theropod.*

Did you know?

Not much is known about *Megalosaurus*, because only fragments of its skeleton have ever been found.

9 metres (29.5 ft) long

Turn to page 160 to see how Megalosaurus fares in battle against Camptosaurus.

Microraptor

*[Microraptor means: **Tiny Hunter**]*

? How do you say it?
My-croh-rap-ter

Microraptor is the smallest known dinosaur. Although it couldn't fly, it had four wings and was so light that it could glide from tree to tree in Early Cretaceous forests. To climb the trees, it would have run up very fast, using its sharp claws to grasp the tree trunk, and its long tail for balance. It probably also flapped its wings to help keep the momentum going.

Dino Fact File

Name: *Microraptor*
Group: Therapod
Discovered: 1999 (China)
Fossils: China
Period: Early Cretaceous
Height: 17 centimetres (6.75 ft)
Length: 77 centimetres (2.5 ft)
Weight: 4.5 kilograms (9.9 lbs)
How it moved: On two legs; gliding
Diet: Carnivorous
Prey: Insects
Main predator: Dilong
Special features: Four wings, like a biplane

Scientists believe Microraptor *had feathers on its legs.*

Did you know?

Until *Microraptor* was discovered, scientists through that *Compsognathus* was the smallest dinosaur.

77 centimetres (2.5 ft) long

Surprise Attack

1 For once, top predator *Neovenator* has under estimated its prey. *Iguanodon* should have been an easy meal, but the herbivore is firmly defending its territory from its attacker.

Iguanodon

Neovenator

2

Iguanodon's thumb-spike pushes deep into the chest of **Neovenator,** making it roar in pain. But can Iguanodon maintain the advantage? Can it really defeat a **Neovenator,** the dinosaur that is its natural predator?

Turn to page 249 to find out.

Neovenator

[*Neovenator* means: **New Hunter**]

? How do you
say it?
Neo-ven-a-tor

Neovenator was discovered on the Isle of Wight in Britain in 1978, but not named until 1996. It was a big, predatory theropod. *Neovenator* was light for its massive size, so it was probably an agile animal. This dangerous dinosaur would have preyed on plant-eaters such as *Iguanodon*. But many of *Neovenator's* fossil bones show signs of healed injuries, suggesting that it did not always escape unhurt.

Dino Fact File

Name: *Neovenator*
Group: Theropod
Discovered: 1978 (England)
Fossils: England
Period: Early Cretaceous
Height: 2.5 metres (8 ft)
Length: 8 metres (26 ft)
Weight: 2,500 kilograms (5,500 lbs)
How it moved: On two legs
Diet: Carnivorous
Prey: *Iguanodon*
Main predator: None
Special features: Teeth so sharp that they could slice through flesh like steak knives

Turn to page 206 to see how *Neovenator* fares in battle against *Iguanodon*.

8 metres (26 ft) long

Neovenator was a top predator of the Cretaceous Period.

Did you know?

When *Neovenator* was discovered, scientists thought it was a new species of *Megalosaurus*.

Olorotitan

[*Olorotitan* means: **Giant Swan**]

? How do you say it?
Oh-low-roh-tie-tan

The duckbills were the main plant-eaters at the end of the Cretaceous period. They are called duckbills because their mouths look like a duck's beak. The beak was used to strip needles from trees. Duckbills had massive chewing teeth that could grind the toughest plant material.

Dino Fact File

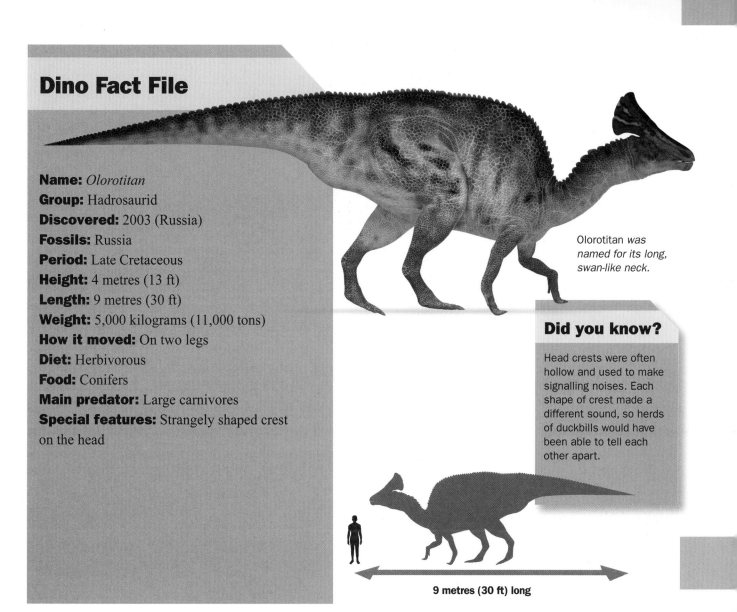

Name: *Olorotitan*
Group: Hadrosaurid
Discovered: 2003 (Russia)
Fossils: Russia
Period: Late Cretaceous
Height: 4 metres (13 ft)
Length: 9 metres (30 ft)
Weight: 5,000 kilograms (11,000 tons)
How it moved: On two legs
Diet: Herbivorous
Food: Conifers
Main predator: Large carnivores
Special features: Strangely shaped crest on the head

Olorotitan was named for its long, swan-like neck.

Did you know?

Head crests were often hollow and used to make signalling noises. Each shape of crest made a different sound, so herds of duckbills would have been able to tell each other apart.

9 metres (30 ft) long

209

Oviraptor

[*Oviraptor* means: **Egg Robber]**

? **How do you say it?** *Oh-vi-rap-ter*

Oviraptor was a dinosaur that looked and acted like a bird. Scientists think it even had feathers! Scientists found a fossil of an *Oviraptor* sitting on a nest. It had its wings spread over some eggs. This showed the scientists that *Oviraptor* sat on its eggs until they hatched. This crest might have been used to signal to other *Oviraptors*. Its strong jaws may have been used for crushing snails or shellfish.

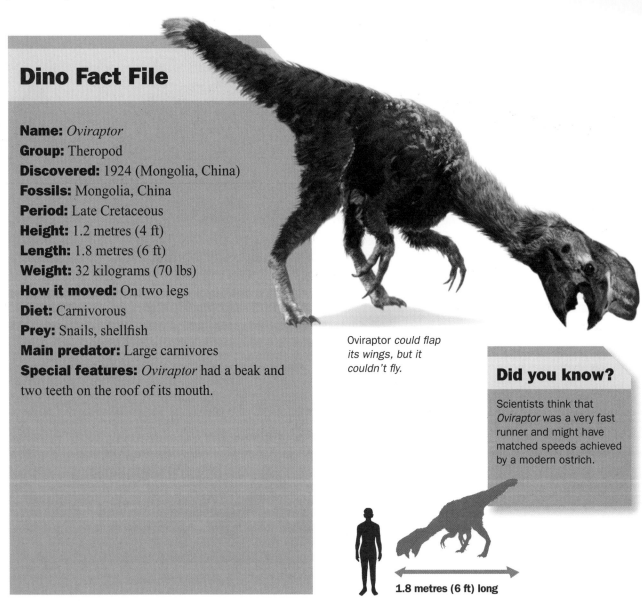

Dino Fact File

Name: *Oviraptor*
Group: Theropod
Discovered: 1924 (Mongolia, China)
Fossils: Mongolia, China
Period: Late Cretaceous
Height: 1.2 metres (4 ft)
Length: 1.8 metres (6 ft)
Weight: 32 kilograms (70 lbs)
How it moved: On two legs
Diet: Carnivorous
Prey: Snails, shellfish
Main predator: Large carnivores
Special features: *Oviraptor* had a beak and two teeth on the roof of its mouth.

Oviraptor could flap its wings, but it couldn't fly.

Did you know?

Scientists think that *Oviraptor* was a very fast runner and might have matched speeds achieved by a modern ostrich.

1.8 metres (6 ft) long

210

Ouranosaurus

[*Ouranosaurus* means: **Brave Monitor Lizard]**

? How do you say it?
Oh-ran-oh-saw-rus

Ouranosaurus belonged to the Iguanodon group of plant-eating dinosaurs and lived on tropical lowland forests and swamps. It had a tall sail running down the length of its back, which scientists think it used to keep cool.

Dino Fact File

Name: *Ouranosaurus*
Group: Iguanodon
Discovered: 1965 (Niger, West Africa)
Fossils: Niger, West Africa
Period: Early Cretaceous
Length: 7 metres (23 ft)
Weight: 2,000 kilograms (44,000 lbs)
How it moved: On all four, but could raise to two
Diet: Herbivorous
Food: Ferns, horsetails
Main predator: *Suchomimus*
Special features: A large sail or fin on its back, thought to help control body temperature

Ouranosaurus *had hoof-like feet, with spiked claws on the thumbs.*

7 metres (23 ft) long

Did you know?

It is thought that *Ouranosaurus* was cold-blooded and would have used its sail to soak up heat from the sun, which could then circulate around the body.

211

Parasaurolophus

[*Parasaurolophus* means: **Near-crested Lizard**]

This curious looking beast was a lambeosaur – a duck-billed, crested dinosaur. The crest contained a series of tubes connecting the nose to the throat. Lambeosaurs probably used their crests to make sounds, perhaps to call to one another. The bones of Parasaurolophus have been found with healed bite marks from predatory dinosaurs, showing that it sometimes escaped its attackers.

How do you say it?

Para-low-four-saw-rus

Dino Fact File

Name: *Parasaurolophus*
Group: Lambeosaur
Discovered: 1922 (New Mexico, USA)
Fossils: North America, Asia
Period: Late Cretaceous
Hip Height: 3.5 metres (11.5 feet)
Length: 10 metres (33 ft)
Weight: 2,500 kilograms (5,511 lbs)
How it moved: On all fours
Diet: Herbivorous
Food: Conifers, seeds, fruit
Main predator: *Tyrannosaurus*
Special features: *Parasaurolophus* had skull like a big bony banana

Parasaurolophus *was both bipedal and quadrepedal.*

Turn to page 186 to see how *Parasaurolophus* fares in battle against *Gorgosaurus*.

Did you know?

Rare *Parasaurolophus* fossils indicate that the fingers were joined by a mitten-like covering skin.

10 metres (33 ft) long

Plateosaurus

[*Plateosaurus* means: **Flat Lizard]**

Plateosaurus was one of the first dinosaurs to be discovered by scientists. Some *Plateosaurus* fossils were found in France in 1837. *Plateosaurus* had a long neck and a small head. It also had a big body. Plants are tough to digest. So plant-eating dinosaurs needed lots of intestines to digest their food. Plant-eating dinosaurs had big bodies so there was room for their long intestines and big stomachs.

Dino Fact File

Name: *Plateosaurus*

Group: Prosauropod

Discovered: 1834 (France)

Fossils: Central and Northern Europe

Period: Late Triassic

Height: 2.5 metres (8 ft)

Length: 7 metres (23 ft)

Weight: 700 kilograms (1,500 lbs)

How it moved: On two legs

Diet: Herbivorous

Food: Plants

Main predator: Large carnivores

Special features: A large body, but a long neck and small head

Did you know?

For many years, scientists thought *Plateosaurus* walked on all fours most of the time, but now there are arguments suggesting it was bipedal.

7 metres (23 ft) long

Most prosauropods walked on all fours.

Protoceratops

[*Protoceratops* means: **First Horned Face**]

How do you say it?
Pro-toe-sera-tops

This small, horned dinosaur is one of the first Ceratopsians, a group that would eventually lead to *Triceratops*. *Protoceratop's* deep skull and massive lower jaws look fierce, but were adapted to cut through the tough vegetation that made up this herbivore's diet. There is strong evidence that *Protoceratops* lived in large groups, especially when nesting. This is no surprise, given that it shared an environment with the fierce Velociraptor!

Turn to page 244 and 246 to see how *Protoceratops* fares in battle against *Velociraptor*.

Dino Fact File

Name: *Protoceratops*
Group: Ceratopsian
Discovered: 1922 (Mongolia, China)
Fossils: Mongolia, China
Period: Late Cretaceous
Hip Height: 1 metre (3.25 ft)
Length: 2 metres (6.5 ft)
Weight: 350 kilograms (770 lbs)
How it moved: On all fours
Diet: Herbivorous
Food: Cycads
Main predator: *Velociraptor*
Special features: A large frill, made of bone and skin, at the back of the skull

Did you know?

Many *Protoceratops* fossils have been found in China, showing the various different stages of development from egg, through baby to male adult.

2 metres (6.5 ft) long

Long legs suggest that Protoceratops was a fast runner.

214

Pterodactylus

[*Pterodactylus* means: **Wing Finger**]

? **How do you say it?** *Ter-oh-dak-tile-us*

Pterodactylus was a member of the pterosaur family. Some **Pterodactylus** were tiny – just the size of a modern-day starling. They ate insects. Some types of **Pterodactylus** were bigger – the size of modern-day eagles. These ones ate fish or small lizards. **Pterodactylus** had a short tail, a furry body and wings made of skin. It also had a long fourth finger on each hand, which made a kind of frame for the wing.

Dino Fact File

Name: *Pterodactylus*
Group: Pterosaur
Discovered: 1770s (Germany)
Fossils: Europe, Tanzania
Period: Late Jurassic
Wingspan: 1.2 metres (4 ft)
Length: 60 centimetres (2 ft)
Weight: 1 kilogram (2 lbs)
How it moved:
Flying
Diet:
Carnivorous
Prey: Small shore creatures
Main predator: Unknown
Special features: Thick fuzz on the neck and back

Pterodactylus *had a rounded crest on the top of its head and a short tail.*

Did you know?

Pterodactylus was not a dinosaur, but a gull-sized reptile that lived at the same time.

Wingspan: 1.2 metres (4 ft)

Quetzalcoatlus

? **How do you say it?**
Kwets-al-co-at-luss

[*Quetzalcoatlus* means: **Flying Snake**]

Quetzalcoatlus was huge – the biggest of all flying reptiles. It was the size of a small plane! Its body was light so it could stay in the air. It probably only weighed the same as one and a half humans. Scientists think *Quetzalcoatlus* flew over water and scooped up prey in its long jaws. Sometimes it ate carrion – that is, animals that were already dead. *Quetzalcoatlus* had good eyesight to see prey far below it.

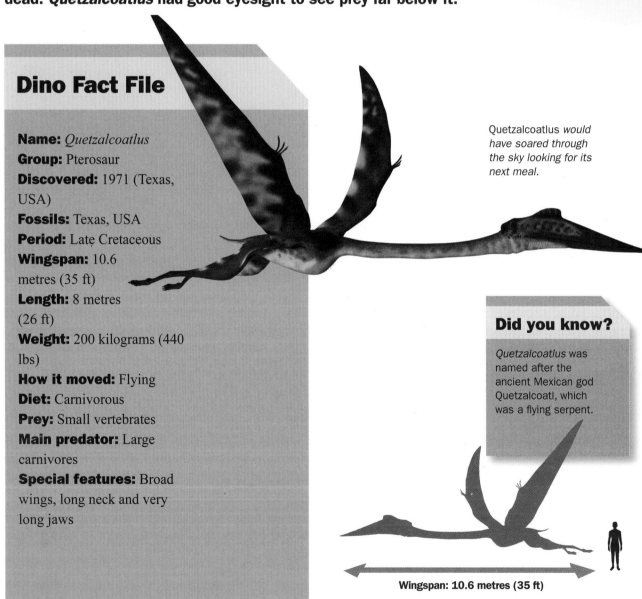

Dino Fact File

Name: *Quetzalcoatlus*
Group: Pterosaur
Discovered: 1971 (Texas, USA)
Fossils: Texas, USA
Period: Late Cretaceous
Wingspan: 10.6 metres (35 ft)
Length: 8 metres (26 ft)
Weight: 200 kilograms (440 lbs)
How it moved: Flying
Diet: Carnivorous
Prey: Small vertebrates
Main predator: Large carnivores
Special features: Broad wings, long neck and very long jaws

Quetzalcoatlus *would have soared through the sky looking for its next meal.*

Did you know?

Quetzalcoatlus was named after the ancient Mexican god Quetzalcoatl, which was a flying serpent.

Wingspan: 10.6 metres (35 ft)

Sauropelta

[*Sauropelta* means: **Shielded Lizard**]

? **How do you say it?** *Saw-ro-pel-ta*

Some plant-eating dinosaurs were covered in armour, like battle tanks! *Sauropelta* was a big, heavy, armoured dinosaur. It weighed the same as three elephants. A predator would break its teeth on *Sauropelta's* armour! The only way to hurt this dinosaur was to flip it over. *Sauropelta's* neck was protected by sharp spikes.

Dino Fact File

Name: *Sauropelta*
Group: Nodosaurid
Discovered: 1930s (Montana, USA)
Fossils: North America
Period: Early Cretaceous
Height: 2 metres (6.5 ft)
Length: 5 metres (16.5 ft)
Weight: 1,500 kilograms (3,300 lbs)
How it moved: On all fours
Diet: Herbivorous
Food: Low-lying vegetation
Main predator: *Deinonychus*
Special features: Long and sturdy neck spikes

Did you know?

Sauropelta's skull was triangular when viewed from above – wider at the rear and tapering towards the snout.

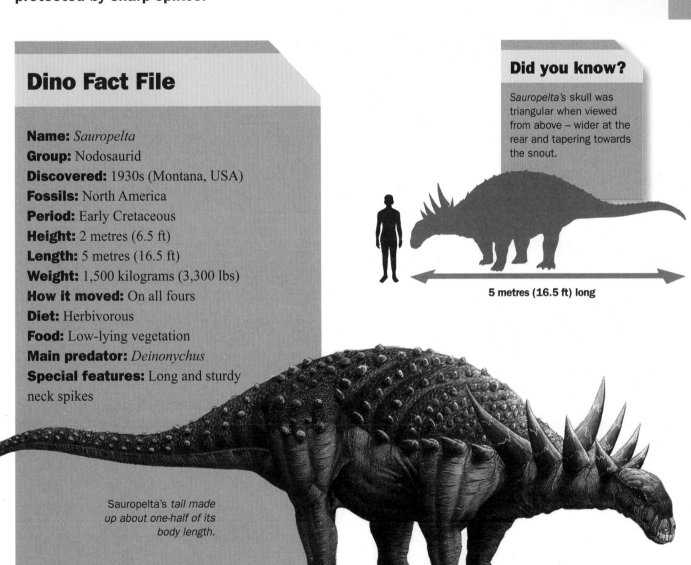

5 metres (16.5 ft) long

Sauropelta's *tail made up about one-half of its body length.*

1 There is enough flesh on that sauropod to keep *Acrocanthosaurus* and its young alive for weeks. Only a bite to the neck will fell the vast titan, and this has to be delivered before *Sauroposeidon* can rear up on its hind legs and bring its vast weight crushing down on the predator.

Sauroposeidon

The Earth Shakes

Acrocanthosaurus

2

Acrocanthosaurus makes its move and breaks its cover. Four tonnes of predator push towards sixty tonnes of prey. The sauropod feels the sudden rush of movement, and instinctively lifts its front limbs while turning towards the blur of motion. The earth shakes as one giant predator and a mountain of prey square up to each other.

Turn to page 249 to find out what happens.

Sauroposeidon ?

[*Sauroposeidon* means: **Lizard Earthquake God**]

How do you say it?
Saw-ro-po-side-on

Sauroposeidon was the tallest animal ever to have lived on planet Earth! *Sauroposeidon* was 21 metres (69 ft) tall – that's the same as four giraffes standing on top of each other! So far, scientists have only found four neck fossils from this dinosaur. They used these fossils to work out its size. *Sauroposeidon* possibly weighed the same as 60 elephants!

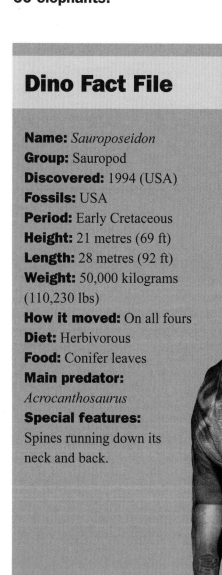

Dino Fact File

Name: *Sauroposeidon*
Group: Sauropod
Discovered: 1994 (USA)
Fossils: USA
Period: Early Cretaceous
Height: 21 metres (69 ft)
Length: 28 metres (92 ft)
Weight: 50,000 kilograms (110,230 lbs)
How it moved: On all fours
Diet: Herbivorous
Food: Conifer leaves
Main predator:
Acrocanthosaurus
Special features:
Spines running down its neck and back.

Turn to page 218 to see how *Sauroposeidon* fares in battle against *Acrocanthosaurus*.

Sauroposeidon's *neck measured 12 metres (40 ft) in length.*

Did you know?

Sauroposeidon's vertebrae (spine bones) had a honeycomb-type formation, with air pockets. This made them light, but also strong.

28 metres (92 ft) long

Scutellosaurus

[*Scutellosaurus* means: **Lizard with Little Shields**]

How do you say it?
Scoo-tell-oh-saw-rus

One of the earliest armoured dinosaurs was *Scutellosaurus*. Its neck, back and long tail were covered in tiny armoured, bonelike shields and its legs were long and thin. In later periods, armoured dinosaurs grew very big, but *Scutellosaurus* was the size of a small dog. *Scutellosaurus* could run on its hind legs, although its armour would have been heavy. It probably spent most of its time on all fours.

Dino Fact File

Name: *Scutellosaurus*
Group: Ornithischian
Discovered: 1981 (Arizona, USA)
Fossils: USA
Period: Early Jurassic
Hip height: 46 centimetres (18 in)
Length: 1.2 metres (4 ft)
Weight: 10 kilograms (22 lbs)
How it moved: On all fours, sometimes raised on two legs
Diet: Herbivorous
Food: Low-growing plants
Main predator: Large predators
Special features: Several different kinds of armour, including oval plates along the side and a ridge of vertical plates down the back and tail

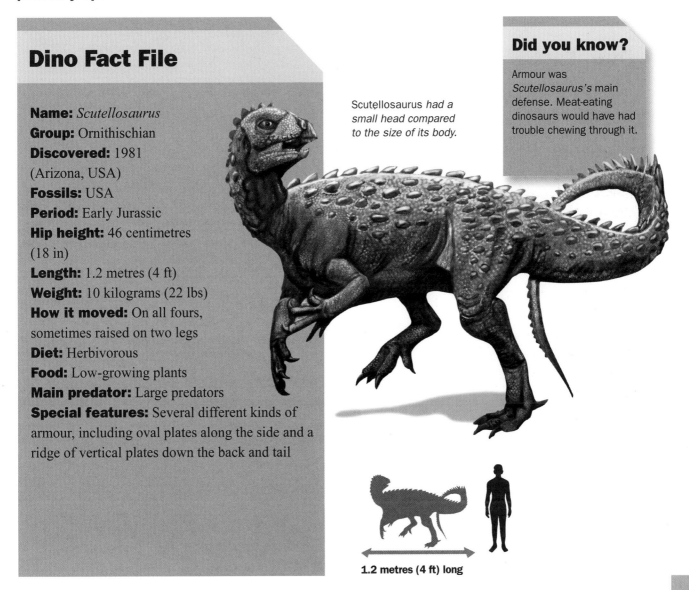

Scutellosaurus *had a small head compared to the size of its body.*

Did you know?

Armour was *Scutellosaurus's* main defense. Meat-eating dinosaurs would have had trouble chewing through it.

1.2 metres (4 ft) long

221

Segnosaurus

[*Segnosaurus* means: **Slow Lizard**]

How do you say it?
Seg-no-saw-rus

Segnosaurus was one of the strangest looking dinosaurs! When scientists found *Segnosaurus* fossils, they found it hard to work out what it looked like. *Segnosaurus* is still a bit of a mystery. But scientists think it had rounded shoulders and big hips. It also had long arms and short legs, like a gorilla or chimpanzee. *Segnosaurus* had huge claws. Maybe they were for digging into insects' nests. Scientists think it was covered in feathers like a bird.

Dino Fact File

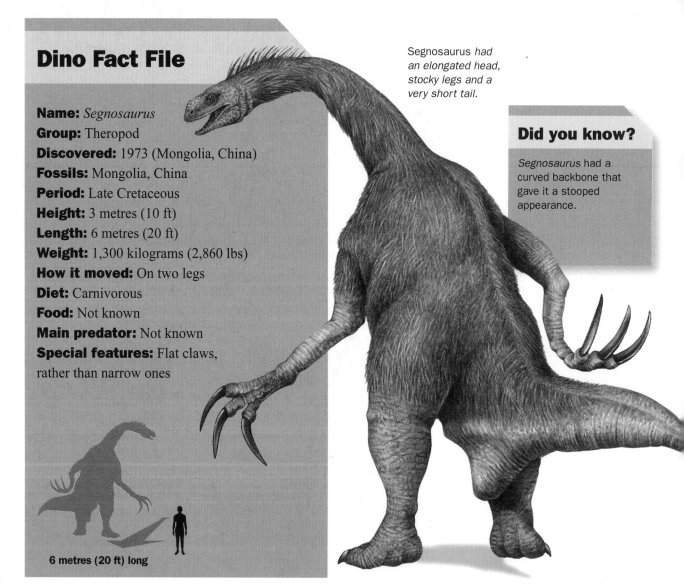

Name: *Segnosaurus*
Group: Theropod
Discovered: 1973 (Mongolia, China)
Fossils: Mongolia, China
Period: Late Cretaceous
Height: 3 metres (10 ft)
Length: 6 metres (20 ft)
Weight: 1,300 kilograms (2,860 lbs)
How it moved: On two legs
Diet: Carnivorous
Food: Not known
Main predator: Not known
Special features: Flat claws, rather than narrow ones

6 metres (20 ft) long

Segnosaurus had an elongated head, stocky legs and a very short tail.

Did you know?

Segnosaurus had a curved backbone that gave it a stooped appearance.

Shonisaurus

[*Shonisaurus* means: **Lizard from the Shoshone Mountains**]

Shonisaurus was the biggest member of the ichthyosaur family. Scientists found one fossil of a *Shonisaurus* that was 21 metres (69 ft) long! That's nearly as big as a blue whale. *Shonisaurus* was a strong swimmer. Its streamlined body helped it to move easily through the water. It had teeth at the front of its snout for grabbing fish.

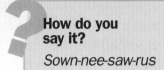

How do you say it?

Sown-nee-saw-rus

Dino Fact File

Name: *Shonisaurus*
Group: Ichthyosaur
Discovered: 1928 (Nevada, USA)
Fossils: USA
Period: Late Triassic
Height: 3 metres (10 ft)
Length: 15 metres (49 ft)
Weight: 30,000 kilograms (66,140 lbs)
How it moved: Swimming
Diet: Piscivorous
Prey: Fish, belemnites
Main predator: Unknown
Special features: Eyeballs as big as the wheel of a car

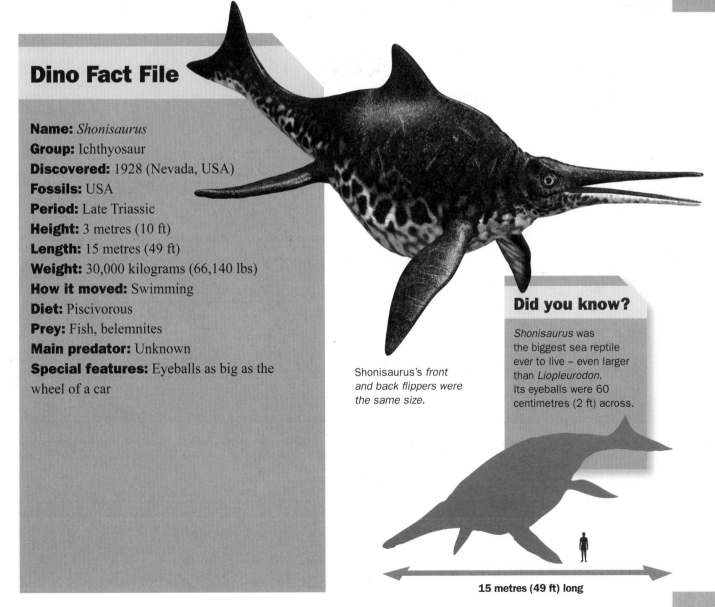

Shonisaurus's *front and back flippers were the same size.*

Did you know?

Shonisaurus was the biggest sea reptile ever to live – even larger than *Liopleurodon*. Its eyeballs were 60 centimetres (2 ft) across.

15 metres (49 ft) long

223

Spinosaurus

[*Spinosaurus* means: **Spine Lizard**]

? **How do you say it?** *Spy-no-saw-rus*

Spinosaurus was a fierce predator that lived in Africa during the mid-Cretaceous period. It has a strange 1.5-metre (5-ft) tall crest along its back that was made of long spines covered by tough skin. This dinosaur had long, narrow jaws lined with razor-sharp, pointed teeth. The design of the jaws and teeth suggest that *Spinosaurus* probably fed mainly on fish that it snatched from rivers and lakes.

Dino Fact File

Name: *Spinosaurus*
Group: Spinosaurid
Discovered: 1912 (Egypt, North Africa)
Fossils: Egypt, Morocco
Period: Late Cretaceous
Hip height: 4.5 metres (14.75 ft)
Length: 16 metres (52.5 ft)
Weight: 7,000 kilograms (15,400 lbs)
How it moved: On two legs, possibly on all fours, too
Diet: Carnivorous
Prey: Fish, dinosaurs, pterosaurs
Main predator: None
Special features: A large spiny sail on its back

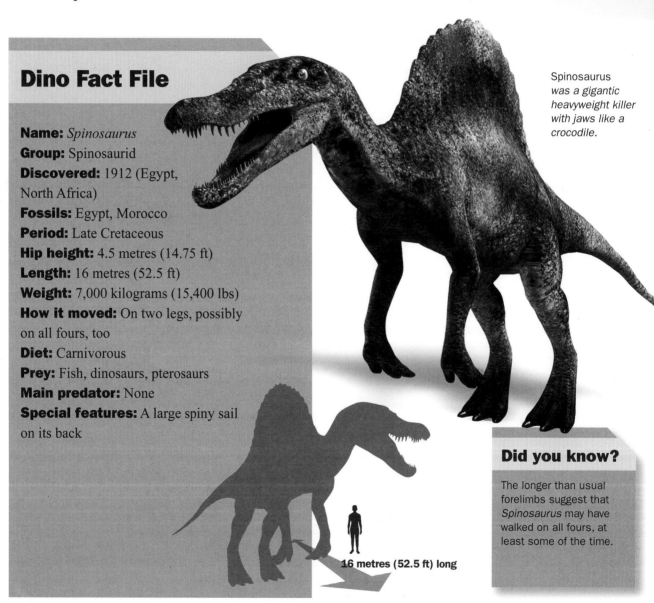

Spinosaurus was a gigantic heavyweight killer with jaws like a crocodile.

16 metres (52.5 ft) long

Did you know?

The longer than usual forelimbs suggest that *Spinosaurus* may have walked on all fours, at least some of the time.

Stegosaurus

[*Stegosaurus* means: **Covered Lizard**]

How do you say it?

Steg-oh-saw-rus

Some herbivores had special body parts to protect them from predators. *Stegosaurus* had plates on its back. Scientists have found fossils of *Stegosaurus* plates, but they don't know for sure how they were arranged. *Stegosaurus* also had four spikes on its tail, which it used to great effect when fighting off carnivores!

Dino Fact File

Name: *Stegosaurus*
Group: Armoured stegosaurid
Discovered: 1877 (Colorado, USA)
Fossils: USA, Portugal
Period: Late Jurassic
Hip height: 2.75 metres (9 feet)
Length: 9 metres (30 ft)
Weight: 1,800 kilograms (4,000 lbs)
How it moved: On all fours
Diet: Herbivorous
Food: Leaves
Main predator: *Allosaurus*
Special features: Bony studs covered the throat like a medieval knight's chain mail

Did you know?

Stegosaurus had leaf-shaped teeth, which were ideal for eating foliage.

9 metres (30 ft) long

Stegosaurus's *front legs were shorter than its back legs*

Stygimoloch

[*Stygimoloch* means: **Horned Devil from the River of Death**]

Stygimoloch came from a group of dinosaurs that scientists call the 'boneheads' which evolved towards the end of the Cretaceous period. *Stygimoloch* had a huge lump of bone in its head. Males used this for head-butting other males in fights over mates. It also had spectacular number of horns around its skull, which made it look bigger and fiercer than it was.

? How do you say it?
Sti-gee-mole-lock

Dino Fact File

Name: *Stygimoloch*
Group: Bonehead
Discovered: 1983
Fossils: Canada; Midwestern USA
Period: Late Cretaceous
Length: 2.7 metres (9 ft)
Weight: 78 kilograms (170 lbs)
How it moved: On two legs
Diet: Herbivorous
Food: Plants
Main predator: *Tyrannosaurus*
Special features: Spikes and spines all around its dome

Stygimoloch *had a stiff, straight tail, which it used for balance.*

Did you know?

The skulls of the boneheads were so solid that they are frequently found as fossils, even thought the rest of the skeleton has long disappeared.

2.7 metres (9 ft) long

Tarbosaurus

[*Tarbosaurus* means: **Alarming Lizard**]

? **How do you say it?** *Tar-bow-saw-rus*

This huge predator from what is now Mongolia would have lived up to its name, alarming lizard. Like most other tyrannosaurs, *Tarbosaurus* was a dangerous predator – it was at the top of the food chain. Its skull was uniquely adapted for making an extra-hard, bone-crushing bite. This could have enabled *Tarbosaurus* to attack prey much larger than itself, maybe even massive sauropods.

Dino Fact File

Name: *Tarbosaurus*
Group: Tyrannosaurid
Discovered: 1946 (Mongolia)
Fossils: Mongolia, China
Period: Late Cretaceous
Height: 4 metres (13 ft)
Length: 12 metres (39 ft)
Weight: 6,000 kilograms (13,200 lbs)
How it moved: On two legs
Diet: Carnivorous
Food: Hadrosaurs, Sauropods
Main predator: None
Special features: Huge hipbones to provide stability for its leg muscles

Did you know?

Tarbosaurus's skull was perfectly adapted to deliver swift, bone-crushing bites.

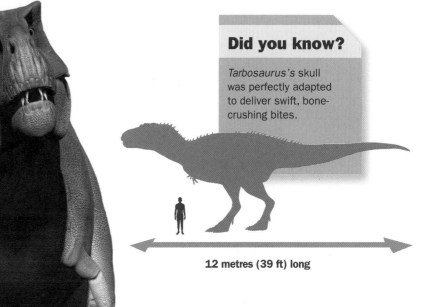

12 metres (39 ft) long

Tarbosaurus *had very short arms, even for a tyrannosaur*

Turn to page 228 to see how *Tarchia* fares in battle against *Tarbosaurus*.

Desert Encounter

1 We are in what is now Mongolia's Gobi Desert, where Cretacaeous dinosaurs are plentiful. This *Tarbosaurus* has approached the heavily armoured *Tarchia* out of curiosity – edging closer to inspect and sniff it.

Tarbosaurus

2 The **Tarchia** becomes irritated with the attention and swiftly turns away, deliberately swinging its heavy tail club at the body of the other animal. Taken by surprise, the predator lifts its right leg to avoid the club and finds itself unbalanced on its left foot.

Tarchia

3 Angry now, the predator lets out a roar, but will it dare to take revenge on the impenetrable creature, or just slope off?

Turn to page 249 to find out.

Tarchia

[*Tarchia* means: **Brainy One**]

? **How do you say it?** *Tah-che-a*

Covered in bony spines, *Tarchia* was an armour-plated tank of a dinosaur. Rows of spikes along its body provided top protection from predators' jaws. Several of the backbones at the end of its tail were enlarged and adapted into a thick, bony club. It would take a very persistent attacker to fight its way past such effective defences!

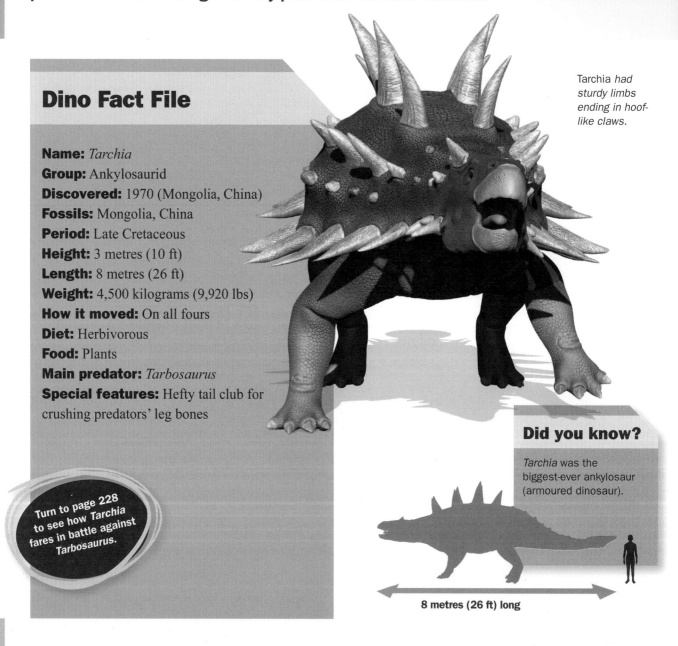

Tarchia had sturdy limbs ending in hoof-like claws.

Dino Fact File

Name: *Tarchia*
Group: Ankylosaurid
Discovered: 1970 (Mongolia, China)
Fossils: Mongolia, China
Period: Late Cretaceous
Height: 3 metres (10 ft)
Length: 8 metres (26 ft)
Weight: 4,500 kilograms (9,920 lbs)
How it moved: On all fours
Diet: Herbivorous
Food: Plants
Main predator: *Tarbosaurus*
Special features: Hefty tail club for crushing predators' leg bones

Turn to page 228 to see how *Tarchia* fares in battle against *Tarbosaurus*.

Did you know?

Tarchia was the biggest-ever ankylosaur (armoured dinosaur).

8 metres (26 ft) long

Tenontosaurus

[*Tenontosaurus* means: **Sinew Lizard** **]**

? How do you say it?

Ten-nont-oh-saw-rus

Tenontosaurus belonged to a group of dinosaurs called the ornithopods, herbivores that thrived in what is now North America during the Cretaceous period. *Tenontosaurus* may have stayed in family groups, possibly as defence against carnivorous attackers such as *Deinonychus*. A gentle beast, *Tenontosaurus* would have spent much of its time chomping on tough plants.

Dino Fact File

Name: *Tenontosaurus*
Group: Ornithopod
Discovered: 1903 (Montana, USA)
Fossils: USA
Period: Late Cretaceous
Height: 2.5 metres (8 ft)
Length: 7 metres (23 ft)
Weight: 900 kilograms (1980 lbs)
How it moved: On all fours
Diet: Herbivorous
Food: Tough plants
Main predator: *Deinonychus*
Special features: A long and broad tail that made up around two-thirds of its body length

Did you know?

Tenontosaurus's back was crisscrossed with a network of bony tendons.

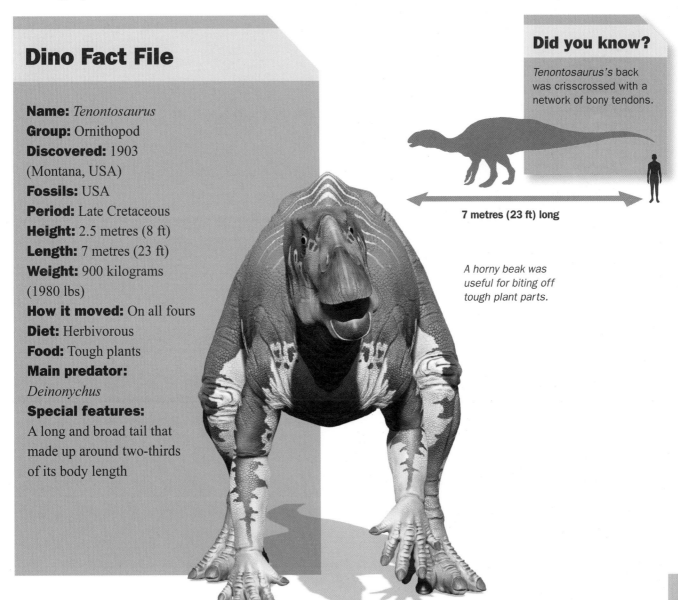

7 metres (23 ft) long

A horny beak was useful for biting off tough plant parts.

231

1 This gentle herbivore's food gathering trip is ending in a meal, but this time *Tenontosaurus* itself is on the menu. The luckless animal steadies itself on all fours as a pack of *Deinonychus* attacks.

Tenontosaurus

Deinonychus

Cretaceous Kill

2 **Tenontosaurus** calls for members of its herd, but its voice is swallowed up by the dense forest. One of the predators grapples for a hold on the tough hide of its prey with its huge second toe-claw.

3 Another circles to the front of the prey to deliver a bite to the throat. Will this flurry of teeth and claws signal the end for **Tenontosaurus**?

Turn to page 249 to find out.

Triceratops

[*Triceratops* means: **Three-horned Face**]

? **How do you say it?** *Tri-sera-tops*

This Late Cretaceous herbivore lived alongside some big predators, including the mighty *T. rex*. The huge frill around the head was a solid sheet of bone crisscrossed by blood vessels. It anchored the huge jaw muscles and might also have helped regulate body temperature, like the bony plates of *Stegosaurus*. The huge belly provided room for a vast stomach to extract the nutrients from its diet of tough plants.

Turn to page 240 to see how *Triceratops* fares in battle against *Tyrannosaurus*.

Dino Fact File

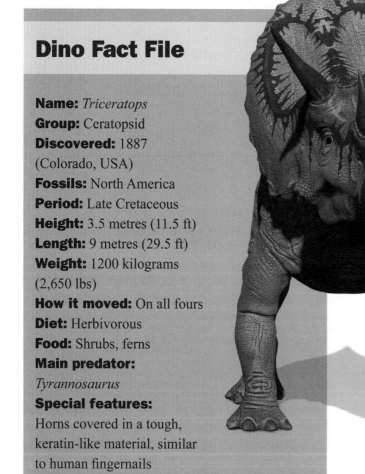

Name: *Triceratops*
Group: Ceratopsid
Discovered: 1887 (Colorado, USA)
Fossils: North America
Period: Late Cretaceous
Height: 3.5 metres (11.5 ft)
Length: 9 metres (29.5 ft)
Weight: 1200 kilograms (2,650 lbs)
How it moved: On all fours
Diet: Herbivorous
Food: Shrubs, ferns
Main predator: *Tyrannosaurus*
Special features: Horns covered in a tough, keratin-like material, similar to human fingernails

Triceratops's *chunky tail houses large muscles.*

Did you know?

Triceratops lived in large herds. If a predator attacked the herd, the adults formed a circle with their horns facing outwards. The babies were safe in the middle of the circle.

9 metres (29.5 ft) long

Troodon

[*Troodon* means: Wounding Tooth]

Troodon was one of the smartest dinosaurs, with a very large brain for its body size. Its name means wounding tooth, after its razor-sharp, saw-edged teeth. Even fossilized ones can be dangerous and palaeontologists have to take extra care when handling them. *Troodon's* large eyes enabled it to see potential prey in dim light, before the prey spotted it, in the shadows of the Cretaceous forests.

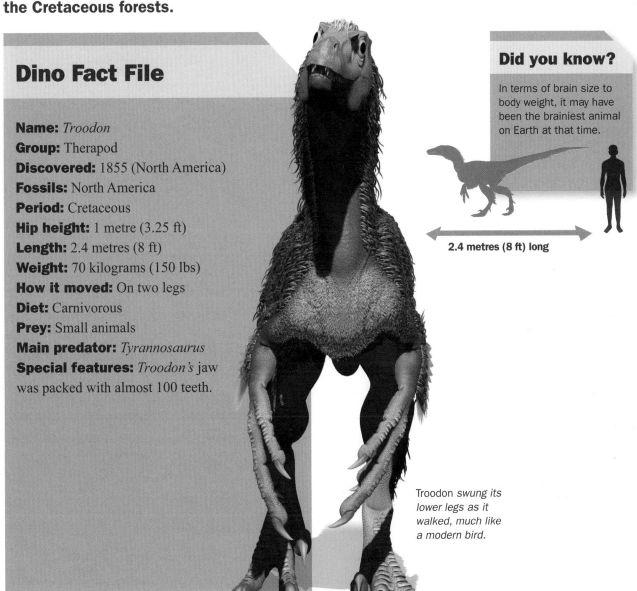

Dino Fact File

Name: *Troodon*
Group: Therapod
Discovered: 1855 (North America)
Fossils: North America
Period: Cretaceous
Hip height: 1 metre (3.25 ft)
Length: 2.4 metres (8 ft)
Weight: 70 kilograms (150 lbs)
How it moved: On two legs
Diet: Carnivorous
Prey: Small animals
Main predator: *Tyrannosaurus*
Special features: *Troodon's* jaw was packed with almost 100 teeth.

Did you know?

In terms of brain size to body weight, it may have been the brainiest animal on Earth at that time.

2.4 metres (8 ft) long

Troodon *swung its lower legs as it walked, much like a modern bird.*

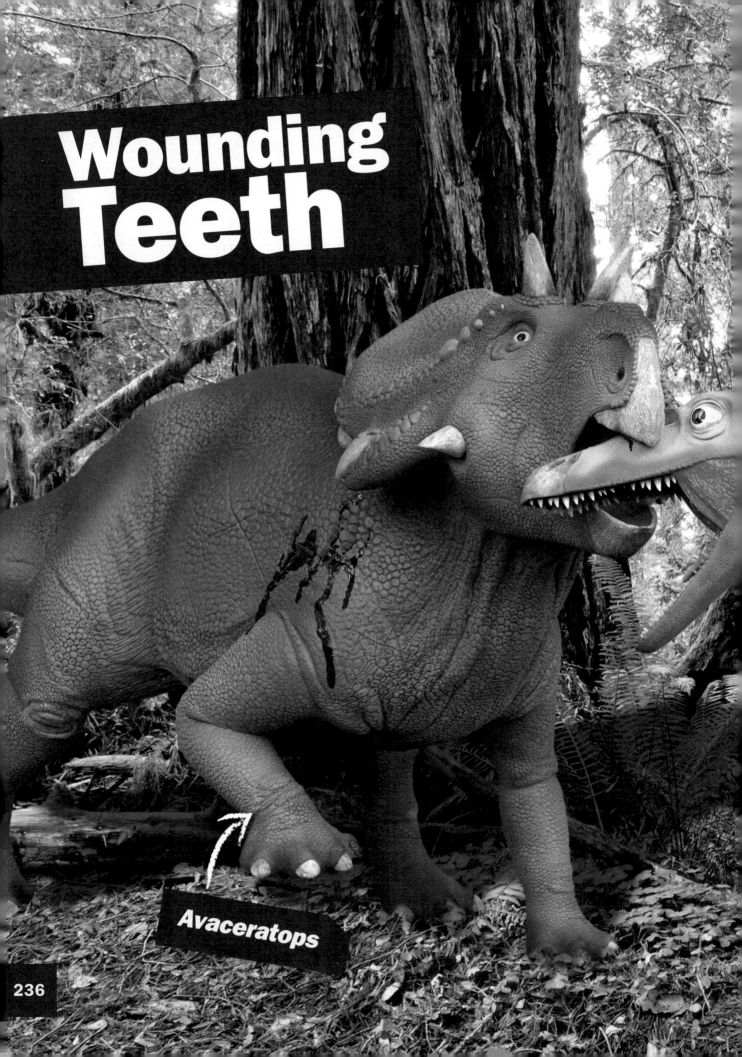

Wounding Teeth

Avaceratops

Troodon

1 It is the Late Cretaceous period and horn-faced dinosaurs dominate the forests of North America. They may be numerous, but they are no match for one particularly intelligent predatory dinosaur, **Troodon**.

2 Just a fraction of the weight of this **Avaceratops**, **Troodon** is nonetheless capable of torturing the horn-face into submission. It darts forwards to peck at the animal's hide again and again, its razor-sharp serrated teeth tearing jagged holes in the **Avaceratop's** flesh. Away from the safety of its herd, the herbivore is paralyzed by fear of this relentless attacker.

Turn to page 249 to find out what happens.

Tylosaurus

[*Tylosaurus* means: **Swollen Lizard**]

? **How do you say it?**
Tie-lo-saw-rus

Tylosaurus was one of a group of swimming reptiles called mosasaurs. These animals had long bodies and a long, flat tail helped them move fast through water when hunting. Mosasaur fossils show these animals were a lot like modern-day lizards. Mosasaurs evolved from lizards that lived on Earth 200 million years ago. *Tylosaurus* ate fish and crunched into prehistoric shellfish called ammonites.

Dino Fact File

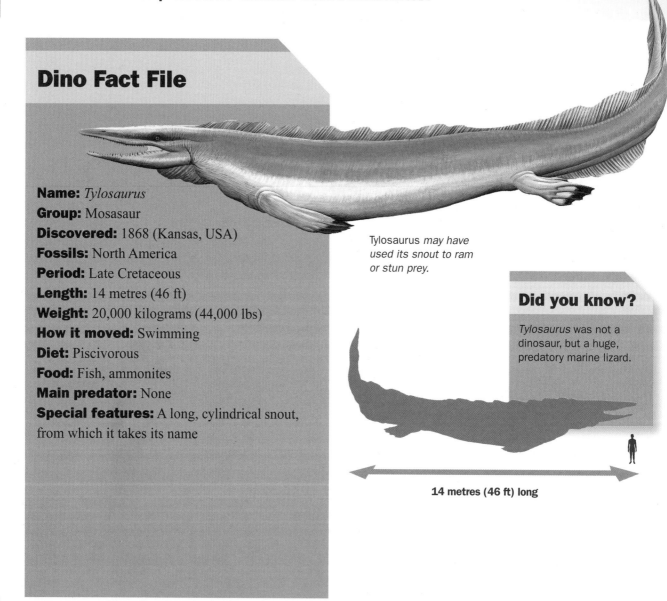

Name: *Tylosaurus*
Group: Mosasaur
Discovered: 1868 (Kansas, USA)
Fossils: North America
Period: Late Cretaceous
Length: 14 metres (46 ft)
Weight: 20,000 kilograms (44,000 lbs)
How it moved: Swimming
Diet: Piscivorous
Food: Fish, ammonites
Main predator: None
Special features: A long, cylindrical snout, from which it takes its name

Tylosaurus *may have used its snout to ram or stun prey.*

Did you know?

Tylosaurus was not a dinosaur, but a huge, predatory marine lizard.

14 metres (46 ft) long

Tyrannosaurus

[*Tyrannosaurus* means: **Tyrant Lizard King**]

? How do you say it?
Tie-ran-oh-saw-rus Rex

The tyrant lizard king is the biggest land predator ever and the world's most famous dinosaur. *T. rex* was as big as an African elephant, could run as fast as an Olympic sprinter, had super senses for hearing, smell and sight and had teeth as long and sharp as carving knives. *T. rex* had a lot of hunting to do – this massive predator would have needed to eat the weight of two human beings every day just to keep going!

Dino Fact File

Name: *Tyrannosaurus*
Group: Tyrannosaurid
Discovered: 1902 (Montana, USA)
Fossils: North America
Period: Late Cretaceous
Hip Height: 5.5 metres (18 ft)
Length: 12 metres (40 ft)
Weight: 6,600 kilograms (14,450 lbs)
How it moved: On two legs
Diet: Carnivorous
Prey: Hadrosaurs, Ceratopsians
Main predator: None
Special features: Biggest and strongest jaws of any dinosaur

Turn to page 240 to see how *Triceratops* fares in battle against *Tyrannosaurus*.

Did you know?

T. rex had a good sense of smell. It could smell a dead animal from kilometres away.

12 metres (40 ft) long

Each of T. rex's *arms could lift up to 400 kilograms (880 lbs).*

Killing **Blow**

1 These titans twist and turn around one another, each trying to deliver the killing blow. **T. rex** is the mightiest predator to have walked the Earth. Its rival is a **Triceratops** – a hulking giant built for both defence and offence. Both animals are fighting fit, but only one will walk away from this battle.

Triceratops

T. Rex

2
Triceratops raises its mighty horns, while pushing its vast bulk towards the ground, presenting its array of horns to **T. rex**. Soon, the tough horns drip with the blood of the attacker. But **T. rex** out-manoeuvres its opponent to get behind **Triceratop's** head-frill, clamping its colossal jaws around the softer neck hide.

Turn to page 249 to find out what happens.

Utahraptor

[*Utahraptor* means: Utah's Predator]

This sickle-clawed dinosaur was named after the US state in which it was discovered. It was the largest member of the dromaeosauridae group – bird-like, bipedal dinosaurs of the Cretaceous period. The claw on its second toe was enlarged into a big, hook-like weapon. *Utahraptor* was an intelligent dinosaur and may have been top predator of its home area.

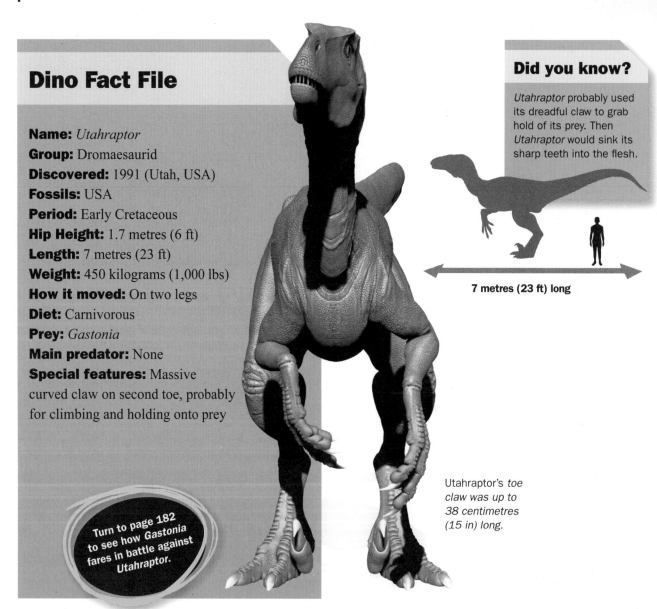

Dino Fact File

Name: *Utahraptor*
Group: Dromaesaurid
Discovered: 1991 (Utah, USA)
Fossils: USA
Period: Early Cretaceous
Hip Height: 1.7 metres (6 ft)
Length: 7 metres (23 ft)
Weight: 450 kilograms (1,000 lbs)
How it moved: On two legs
Diet: Carnivorous
Prey: *Gastonia*
Main predator: None
Special features: Massive curved claw on second toe, probably for climbing and holding onto prey

Turn to page 182 to see how *Gastonia* fares in battle against *Utahraptor*.

Did you know?

Utahraptor probably used its dreadful claw to grab hold of its prey. Then *Utahraptor* would sink its sharp teeth into the flesh.

7 metres (23 ft) long

Utahraptor's *toe claw was up to 38 centimetres (15 in) long.*

Velociraptor

*[Velociraptor means: **Speedy Thief**]*

Velociraptor was a feathered dinosaur that lived in Asia towards the end of the Cretaceous period. It had about 80 teeth that were designed for ripping and tearing flesh. Narrow jaws allowed *Velociraptor* to push its head inside the carcass of a dinosaur. It attacked with the claws of all four limbs and could even jump up onto the back of its prey.

How do you say it?

Vel-oh-sir-rap-tor

Turn to page 244 to see how *Velociraptor* fares in battle against *Protoceratops*.

Dino Fact File

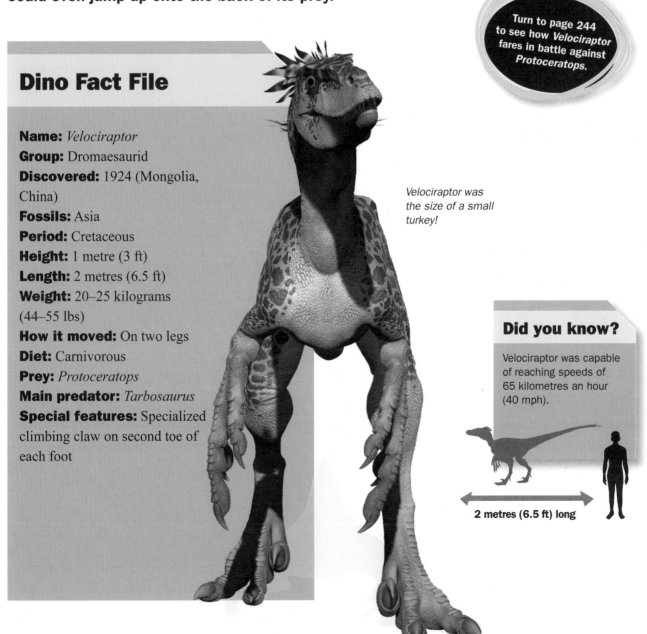

Name: *Velociraptor*
Group: Dromaesaurid
Discovered: 1924 (Mongolia, China)
Fossils: Asia
Period: Cretaceous
Height: 1 metre (3 ft)
Length: 2 metres (6.5 ft)
Weight: 20–25 kilograms (44–55 lbs)
How it moved: On two legs
Diet: Carnivorous
Prey: *Protoceratops*
Main predator: *Tarbosaurus*
Special features: Specialized climbing claw on second toe of each foot

Velociraptor was the size of a small turkey!

Did you know?

Velociraptor was capable of reaching speeds of 65 kilometres an hour (40 mph).

2 metres (6.5 ft) long

1 A **Protoceratops** mother and her young concentrate on consuming another tough meal. So much chewing and grinding for so little nourishment. But they will soon have greater worries than finding their next meals, for their search for food has led them into **Velociraptor** territory.

Protoceratops

Under Cover

Velociraptor

2 Even now, two of the predators are creeping towards the herbivores. They would not take on an adult **Protoceratops**, but the young are another matter. Without making a sound, the crafty carnivores slowly and deliberately move to an attack position...

3 Seeing a flash of claws and teeth, the **Protoceratopses** react fast – and run for their lives. The chase begins, but inevitably the young can't keep up with its mother. The infant herbivore is snapped up and carried off. The mother turns to give chase, and finds itself face-to-face with another predator.

Velociraptor

The Fight Back

Protoceratops

4

With a bellow of fury, the **Protoceratops** launches an attack, biting down hard on the **Velociraptor's** arm. The aggressor responds by frantically stabbing at the **Protoceratops's** belly with its sickle-shaped claw. Can the herbivore manoeuvre its superior body weight to crush its foe? Or will the **Velociraptor** come out on top?

Turn to page 249 to find out what happens.

Battle
Winners and Losers

Which of these **titans** won the war? Who was **meat**, who **lived** to fight another day, and who was a true **victor**?

Predator Trap
Allosaurus vs Stegosaurus
page 150

After a long battle, *Stegosaurus's* crushed skull proved fatal. A wounded *Allosaurus* was the victor.

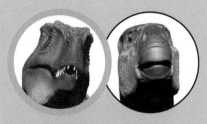

Cornered
Megalosaurus vs Camptosaurus page 160

The superior strength and speed of *Megalosaurus* won over and it was toast for *Camptosaurus*.

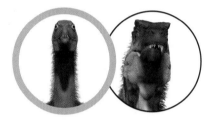

Clashing Cousins
Archaeopteryx vs Compsognathus page 166

Of these two weeds, *Compsognathus* was the stronger animal, but *Archaeopteryx* could simply fly away!

Fresh Meat
Dilophosaurus vs Anchisaurus page 172

The slowest of those, *Anchisaurus* was felled by the crested beast. Fresh meat for *Dilophosaurus*!

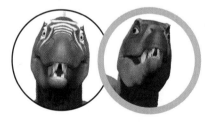

Jaws
Herrerasaurus vs Eoraptor
page 178

Eoraptor didn't have the strength and mass of its predator, but it was fast enough to escape *Herrerasaurus*.

Claws on Armour
Utahraptor vs Gastonia
page 182

Utahraptor used its superior battle skills to pierce *Gastonia's* spiky defence to overcome the hapless herbivore.

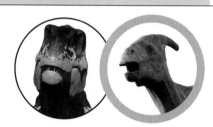

The Last Lunge
Gorgosaurus vs Parasaurolophus page 186

That old *Gorgosaurus* was on its last legs. The herd easily fought it off and continued with their mission.

In For The Kill
Albertosaurus vs Hypacrosaurus page 194

No question of the outcome here! *Hypacrosaurus* was quickly turned into a fine feast for the carnivores.

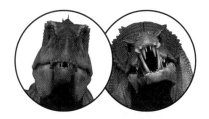

Crocodile Jaws
Carcharadontosaurus vs Kaprosuchus page 200

Carcharadontosaurus was too heavy to drag into the water to drown, so *Kaprosuchus* had to abandon its prey. No winner – or loser – in this battle.

Surprise Attack
Iguanodon vs Neovenator page 206

For once, *Neovenator* loped off licking its wounds! *Iguanodon* was the unlikely victor of this battle.

The Earth Shakes
Sauroposeidon vs Acrocanthosaurus page 218

Even 60,000 kilograms of sauropod could not stand up to top predator *Acrocanthosaurus*.

Desert Encounter
Tarbosaurus vs Tarchia page 228

A surprise result for low-scoring *Tarchia*. The armoured dino scared the tyrannosaur into making a retreat.

Cretaceous Kill
Tenontosaurus vs Deinonychus page 232

Poor *Tenontosaurus* didn't stand a chance against a pack of fierce *Deinonychus*.

Wounding Teeth
Troodon vs Avaceratops page 236

Troodon succeeded in severely wounding the terrified *Avaceratops*. Then it left the herbivore to become easy prey for bigger carnivores.

Killing Blow
T. rex vs Triceratops page 240

Triceratops put up a brave fight, but did he ever really stand a chance? No dinosaur, not even three-horned-face, gets to lick the T!

The Fight Back
Velociraptor vs Protoceratops page 246

Two losers! Both the battling dinosaurs died in a fatal embrace.

Glossary

Ammonite

An extinct marine mollusc with a spiral shell, found as fossils in rocks that date from the Jurassic and Cretaceous periods.

Amphibian

An animal that can live both on land and in water. Frogs and toads are amphibians.

Ankylosaurs

A group of armour-plated herbivorous dinosaurs that appeared in the Jurassic period and persisted until the end of the Cretaceous period.

Biped

An animal that walks on its hind-legs and does not use its arms in locomotion.

Carnivore

An animal that eats mostly meat – dead or alive.

Ceratopsians

A group of dinosaurs that includes *Triceratops* and all its horned and beak-faced relations.

Conifer tree

An evergreen tree that has small, tough, needle-like leaves.

Continent

One of the world's main, big, continuous areas of land.

Cretaceous period

Lasted from 145–66 million years ago and represents the last period of time in which dinosaurs dominated the Earth.

Cycad

A tall, palm-like plant that can be found in tropical regions.

Denticles

Small bony plates that can form within or on the surface of an animal's skin.

Dromaeosaurids

A distinct family of bird-like predatory dinosaurs that became common in the Late Cretaceous period.

Duckbill

A nickname for hadrosaur dinosaurs after their broad mouth that resembled the bill of a very large duck!

Erosion

The gradual wearing away of rocks or soil.

Evolution

Changes or developments that happen to all forms of life over millions of years, as a result of changes in the environment.

Extinct

The global and total loss of multiple or single species on Earth.

Fern

A flowerless plant that has feathery or leafy fronds.

Food chain

The relationship of what is eaten and the links between species in a distinct environment.

Fossil

The preserved remains (such as bones and teeth) or traces (such as tracks) of life on Earth.

Fossil record
All the known fossils through geological time.

Fossil specimen
A single fossil that might be studied by a palaeontologist.

Herbivore
An animal that only eats plants in its diet.

Horsetail
A flowerless plant with a hollow, jointed stem.

Hunting ground
An area where an animal hunts its prey.

Ichthyosaurs
A group of swimming reptiles from the Mesozoic era. They had fishlike bodies and tail fins.

Invertebrate
An animal that doesn't have a spine.

Jurassic Period
Lasted from 201–145 million years ago and marks the time (175 million years ago) when the supercontinent Pangaea started to break-up.

Lambeosaurs
A group of late Cretaceous herbivorous hadrosaur dinosaurs that often sported crests upon their heads.

Marsupial
An animal, such as a kangaroo, that has a pouch on the front of its body in which it carries its young.

Mesozoic Era
The time between 251–66 million years ago, which scientists divide into three periods, the Triassic, Jurassic and Cretaceous. The Mesozoic Era is sometimes called The Age of the Dinosaurs.

Mosasaur
A member of a group of big swimming reptiles of the Cretaceous period, closely related to modern-day lizards.

Nesting
An animal that builds a structure in which to raise its young. Birds build nests from twigs and leaves and dinosaurs kicked earth into a mound.

Ornithischian
Means 'bird-hipped' and is applied to all dinosaurs that had a distinct bone structure to their hips, which looked like a birds' hips, but these dinosaurs did not give rise to birds!

Ornithopods
A hugely successful group of herbivorous ornithischian dinosaurs.

Pack-hunter
A predator that actively works with members of its own species to hunt and attack prey.

Palaeontologist
A scientist who studies the traces and fossil remains of extinct plants and animals.

Pangaea
One massive continent that covered the Earth from 300 million years ago until its break up around 175 million years ago.

Plesiosaur
A large marine reptile of the Mesozoic Era, with large, paddlelike limbs and a long flexible neck.

Pliosaur
A plesiosaur with a short neck, large head and massive toothed jaws.

Predator
An animal that actively hunts, captures and eats other animals.

Prosauropod
Late Triassic period ancestors of long-necked, plant-eating dinosaurs.

Prey
An animal that is hunted and eaten by predators.

Pterosaur
One of a group of flying reptiles from the Mesozoic Era. They had leathery wings supported by an elongated finger.

Quadruped
An animal that walks using both its arms and legs, literally on all fours.

Reptile
A group of animals that became adapted to lay eggs on land and survive in harsher conditions than their water-based ancestors.

Saurischian
Means 'lizard-hipped' and refers to a group that includes the sauropod and theropod dinosaurs.

Sauropod
Saurischian herbivores with long necks, small heads, long tails and large quadrupedal bodies.

Sediment
Matter carried by water or wind and then laid on the land or seabed.

Sedimentary
A type of rock that formed from sediment.

Species
A distinct group of plants or animals that can reproduce to create offspring.

Stegosaurs
A group of dinosaurs with rows of bony plates or spines running down their backs.

Territory
A discrete area within an environment where an animal claims to live and often defends from competing members of its own and other species.

Theropod
This name literally means 'beast-foot' and is applied to all predatory dinosaurs and their descendants, the birds!.

Triassic period
Lasted from 252–201 million years ago and marks the first appearance of dinosaurs.

Tyrannosaur
A term used to group together close relatives of *Tyrannosaurus*, such as *Tarbosaurus*.

Vertebrate
An animal with a backbone.

Index

Acknowledgements

Illustrations: John Alston, Lisa Alderson, Dougal Dixon, Simon Mendez, Luis Rey

Alamy: 11 (b) Jack Carey; 21 (c) MERVIN REES; 25 (cr), 63 (t), 65 (t), 77 (t), 95 (c), 118, 125 (t) The Natural History Museum; 71 (tl) Stocktrek Images, Inc.; 88 (t) Robert E. Barber; 95 (t) Dorset Media Service; 109 (b) Corbin17; 119 (t) Pictorial Press Ltd; 137 (t) Lou-Foto.

Corbis: 6 (bl), 7 (br), 120 (t), 123 (t), 126 (t) Jonathan Blair; 9 (br), 49 (c), 135 (c) Louie Psihoyos; 35 (br) Paul Souders; 52 (b) Leonello Calvetti; 79 (t), 133 (t) Ken Lucas; 93 (bl) Kevin Shafer; 120 (b), 126 (b) Ingo Arndt; 135 (t) James L. Amos; 137 (b) Nobumichi Tamura; 211 Craig Brown.

Getty Images: 11 (t) SSPL; 11 (c) John Downes, Dorling Kindersley; 35 (t) Colin Keates, Dorling Kindersley; 51 (c) Simon Roulstone, Dorling Kindersley; 57 (b) ullstein bild; 117 (c) De Agostini Picture Library; 139 (t) O. Louis Mazzatenta, National Geographic; 139 (r) Dorling Kindersley; 160 Dorling Kindersley RF; 226 Mohamad Haghani/Stocktrek Images, Inc.

Shutterstock: 18–19 Kostyantyn Ivanyshen; 21 (br) Michael Rosskothen; 33 (l) Chris Fourie; 33 (r) Worakit Sirijinda; 35 (bl) THPStock; 37 (c) Tao Jiang; 48, 58, 105 (b), 132, 203 Michael Rosskothen; 59 (t), 136 (b), 142–143 Elenarts; 60–61 Computer Earth; 65 (b) yankane; 67 (b) schankz; 72 (br), 97 (t), 98–99, 129, 202, 205, 209 Catmando; 75 (c), 174 Ozja; 75 (t) B. and E. Dudzinscy; 77 (c) Sarah Jessup; 79 (b), 122, 223 Linda Bucklin; 81 (t) Oleg Znamenskiy; 87 (b) nouseforname; 89 (t) Achimdiver; 93 (t) worldswildlifewonders; 95 (b) MAHATHIR MOHD YASIN; 104 (c), 107 (t) Russell Shively; 107 (br) Pictries; 115 (t) ChinellatoPhoto; 123 (c) Eric Isselee; 127 (c) Igor Chernomorchenko; 144 (bl) MarcelClemens; 159 Bob Orsillo; 164 DM7.

Wikimedia Commons: 87 (t) ДиБгд; 117 (t), 117 (b) Ghedoghedo.

Publisher: Samantha Warrington

Art director: Miranda Snow

Managing editor: Karen Rigden

Production controller: Sarah-Jayne Johnson

Designer: Leah Germann

Editor: Anna Southgate

Some of this material appeared previously in *Deadly Animals*, *Dinosaur Wars*, *Dinosaurs Dominate*, *My First Book of Dinosaurs*, *T. Rex is King* and *The Ultimate Book of Dinosaurs*.